MAINSTREAM PRIMARY SCHOOLING
YOUR SPECIAL-NEEDS CHILD

PRAISE

An informative and practical guide that honestly depicts the challenges and joys of navigating the mainstream school system with your special-needs child. A brilliant read for parents/carers and teachers alike.

Luca Dickinson, classroom teacher

An extremely straightforward and insightful guide for families navigating their 'new normal'. You can pick up Alicia's book and read the chapter that relates to your current time and challenges – like a checklist for navigating the early years.

Rebecca Mercuri, We Rock the Spectrum sensory-safe gym

As an experienced educator, I've spent years working in schools, but nothing prepared me for the emotional intensity of navigating mainstream education as a parent of a child with additional needs. The rules felt different, the stakes felt higher, and the path was anything but clear. Alicia's writing gently lit the way forward, offering practical support, heartfelt encouragement and the deep reassurance that I wasn't alone.

Meg Durham, mother, podcaster and wellbeing specialist

This book is an incredible resource for anyone negotiating mainstream education for children with additional needs. It offers a diverse range of much-needed perspectives, including stories from parents and educators that show we're not alone and we can make it through the tough times. As an educator and a parent myself, this is an essential read.

Leon Furze, author, educator, parent

MAINSTREAM PRIMARY SCHOOLING

A Parent's Guide to Advocating and Navigating the System

YOUR SPECIAL-NEEDS CHILD

Alicia Cohen

Published in 2025 by Amba Press, Melbourne, Australia
www.ambapress.com.au

© Alicia Cohen 2025

All rights reserved. No part of this book may be reproduced or transmitted in any form or by any means, electronic or mechanical, including photocopying, recording or by any information storage and retrieval system, without prior permission in writing from the publisher.

Cover design: Tess McCabe
Internal design: Amba Press
Editor: Brooke Lyons

ISBN: 9781923403109 (pbk)
ISBN: 9781923403116 (ebk)

A catalogue record for this book is available from the National Library of Australia.

CONTENTS

Introduction: Finding your Path		1
Chapter 1	Choosing to Mainstream your Child	11
Chapter 2	Knowing your Rights	25
Chapter 3	Starting School	41
Chapter 4	Goals	55
Chapter 5	Creating a Team	65
Chapter 6	The 'Professionals'	77
Chapter 7	Managing All the Things	87
Chapter 8	Finding a Tribe	103
Chapter 9	The Tough Times	115
Chapter 10	You	129
Conclusion		141
References		143
Key Contacts		145
About the Author		147

INTRODUCTION
FINDING YOUR PATH

There is nothing like the moment of having a suspected diagnosis confirmed. The future you imagined suddenly shifts, and you find yourself at the beginning of an unexpected journey. The roadmap you thought you'd follow – including how your child would transition to school and the educational choices you'd make – transforms into something entirely different. What once seemed like simple decisions now become complex considerations that touch every aspect of your child's development and wellbeing.

Approaching primary school with a special-needs child requires an enormous amount of research, planning and advocacy. It is a time of heightened emotions that will test and transform you and your family in ways you could never have imagined.

The decision to mainstream your child is perhaps one of the most significant you will make. It's filled with hope, doubt and countless questions: Will they thrive or merely survive?

Will they make friends? Will teachers understand them? Will the school truly accommodate their needs? These questions keep us awake at night as we decide what's best for our children.

As parents, we bring our own educational experiences to the table. Most of us carry vivid memories of our primary school years – the excursions we went on, the teachers who inspired us, the friendships formed in playgrounds.

School has changed dramatically since we were children. The curriculum is fuller, teaching methods have evolved, and thankfully, schools are generally more inclusive. Yet our own experiences inevitably colour our expectations and fears for our children.

Mainstreaming your special-needs child is not for the faint-hearted. It requires thought, work and persistent advocacy. But the rewards – seeing your child participate in school events, learn to read, make friends or achieve goals that once seemed impossible – bring a special kind of joy that parents on this path understand deeply.

This book isn't about finding perfection – nothing is perfect. It's about creating a fulfilling educational experience for your child while preserving your sanity and finding moments of celebration along the way. It's about building a community that understands and supports both you and your child through this journey.

Why I wrote this book

My life changed when we received our child's diagnosis, and it continued to shift in unexpected ways as the years unfolded.

When he was two-and-a-half our firstborn, Remy, was struggling to say words. The kindergarten educator suggested he see a speech pathologist who, after a session or two, recommended we visit a paediatrician. We waited a few months to see one, and from the moment we walked in the door for that first appointment, our family and lives changed.

Remy was diagnosed on the spot with autism spectrum disorder (ASD). Through the extensive diagnosis process it was confirmed as ASD level 3 with an intellectual disability and severe communication challenges.

Remy's diagnosis came as a surprise to me and is something I have found difficult to discuss over the years (maybe that is why I am writing about it instead). When we first received the diagnosis, I understood its significance, but many well-meaning people would say, 'Oh, he'll be high-functioning' without really understanding what that means or the reality of what we were dealing with. I have also heard people say, 'Everyone's a little bit autistic', which is not only inaccurate but undermines the significant challenges we face. These comments, though often well-intentioned, can feel dismissive of our lived experience.

My husband had some disability in his extended family, so he entered this journey with slightly more awareness than I did. In contrast, I have had to learn everything from scratch. I have discovered how much I didn't know and how much I still have to learn. While I tend to avoid well-intentioned but sometimes overwhelming Facebook groups, I do read widely in this area, both for personal understanding and professional knowledge. The learning curve has been steep, but necessary, and continues to evolve as my child grows and his needs change.

The early days after diagnosis were consumed with early intervention and following professional recommendations. We got on to the National Disability Insurance Scheme (NDIS) fairly swiftly and started early intervention with speech pathology and occupational therapy (OT). As the mother, and an organised one at that, I became the one coordinating everything – the appointments, the therapies, the paperwork – all while working full-time. Over time, my work and career had to evolve, sometimes by conscious choice and sometimes because circumstances pushed me onto a different path. I rebranded myself professionally and changed my work significantly to ensure I could be at the school gate every morning and afternoon. Though there were tough times, I prioritised our family over traditional career progression.

A few years after Remy's diagnosis, when we felt more settled in our new reality, we were ready for another child. Remy now has a younger sister, which has brought additional joy and complexity to our family dynamics.

Remy attended both mainstream and special kinder programs. He got so much from the various programs he attended. We also appreciated the communities that both offered us, especially as we were coming to terms with Remy's diagnosis and working out what was going to be the best path for him.

My husband and I felt passionately about Remy attending a mainstream school. We had both gone to the local primary school and felt that the world had changed a lot since we went to school. In all honesty, we thought being around children who talked would encourage him to talk more (spoiler alert – it hasn't). We wanted the most typical childhood possible for him, believing that a more 'normal' childhood would lead to a more normal life.

With my mother having been a high school teacher, I have always deeply valued education. I loved school growing up and fantasised about my own children having that same positive experience. We wanted him to have local friends and that picture-perfect primary school experience that many parents dream of.

We have had a great primary school experience for Remy. Seriously, great, but not perfect – nothing is perfect.

Over the years, many people have asked me about our experience as either their child is about to go through it, or from a general interest perspective. I have met a variety of parents in different stages of this journey who are having a variety of different experiences.

So many factors have played a part in Remy's school experience – from the great teachers he has been lucky enough to have, the friends he has made, to the school itself, to the professionals who have supported him and us, his parents. I thought I would share some of the lessons we have learned over the years and how we have made the experience work for us.

What you will find in this book

This book was written for parents and caregivers of special-needs and additional-needs children. It will be relevant to parents of children with or who are suspected to have attention deficit hyperactivity disorder (ADHD), autism spectrum disorder (ASD), developmental coordination disorder (DCD)/

dyspraxia, dyslexia, dyscalculia and dysgraphia. It will also be relevant to parents of children with additional speech, language and communication needs; developmental delays; physical disabilities (mobility, fine motor skills, visual impairments and hearing impairments); medical conditions such as epilepsy, diabetes and asthma; chronic fatigue syndrome; and mental health conditions including anxiety, depression and obsessive-compulsive disorder (OCD).

This book is for parents and caregivers who are considering mainstream primary schooling (public, catholic or independent) or those who are already mainstreaming their child.

I hope you will find in this book:

- A cheerleader who says if you want to do this, you can
- Many practical tips and ideas relevant to your experience
- Words of wisdom by others who are mainstreaming their special-needs children or working in this area.

This book is not an exhaustive guide, but I hope it covers the main things you will deal with during the experience. I've written about the topics I talk about in detail with other parents in my life; the things I would want to share with a friend who has a special-needs child who is about to start mainstream schooling.

Throughout this book, I've chosen to use terms such as 'special needs' and 'neurodiversity' more frequently than 'disability'. This choice doesn't aim to minimise or deny the real challenges your child faces, but rather recognises that many parents reading this book may be at different stages of their journey.

Coming to terms with your child's diagnosis often involves a gradual process of understanding and acceptance. The word 'disability' can feel confronting when you're still processing what your child's condition means for their future. This isn't about avoiding reality or engaging in euphemisms. This book is about meeting parents where they are in their journey.

As you and your child grow in confidence and understanding, your relationship with terminology may evolve. Many families eventually embrace disability-first language – which emphasises the disability as a central part of a person's identity – as part of accepting and advocating for their child's needs. Whatever terms resonate most with you and your family are valid.

Accepting your child's diagnosis

Everyone processes the news of a diagnosis differently, and there is no right or wrong way to handle it. As I found in my own experience, I needed time to process (and, depending on the day, I might say I am still processing it!) before sharing the news with others. I consciously chose not to dive into Google searches or Facebook groups immediately. Instead, I focused on accepting and understanding my new reality and getting on with supporting my child.

One book that profoundly resonated was *Special* by Australian mother and journalist Melanie Dimmitt. Melanie captures how parenting a child with special needs, while different from what we might have expected, is filled with its own joys and meaningful moments. Her insights help illuminate how you can find contentment and purpose in this altered life path, showing that while it may not be what you planned, it can be equally rich and fulfilling.

The reality is that the diagnosis itself won't change, so the sooner you can come to terms with it, the better it is for everyone involved – especially your child. This doesn't mean you are giving up; rather, it means you are choosing to channel your energy into productive actions and support. Like many parents who are on this journey, I had minimal experience or knowledge of the realities of disability before my child was diagnosed so this has all been a learning experience for me.

Each day brings its own challenges and wins. Accepting your child's diagnosis allows you to be more present for both celebrating the positives and navigating the difficulties with greater resilience.

PARENT INSIGHT

No one believed me at first. My child was thriving at school – engaged, bright, well-behaved. Teachers praised her focus and adaptability. Friends and family reassured me, saying, 'She's fine! You're overthinking it.' But they didn't see what happened when we got home.

Home was where the mask came off. After holding it together all day in the structured, predictable environment of school, my child would walk through the door and unravel. The meltdowns, the explosive emotions, the exhaustion – all of it saved just for me, their safe place. I was the one they could fall apart on. I was the one absorbing their pain, their sensory overload, their frustration. And yet, to the outside world, everything seemed fine.

The journey to getting answers was exhausting. Appointment after appointment, assessments, follow-ups, waiting lists that felt endless. At each step I was met with doubt – by doctors, by family members, even sometimes by myself. Was I imagining this? Was I the problem? But deep down, I knew. I knew this wasn't just 'bad behaviour' or 'a phase'.

The silent struggle of advocating for your neurodiverse child is isolating. You become their voice, their shield, their anchor. You battle systems that aren't built for them, all while managing the emotional toll at home. And still, you love them fiercely. You learn their triggers, their needs, their language. You build them a world where they feel safe, understood and accepted – even if it means taking the brunt of their hardest moments.

Because at the end of the day, no matter how hard it gets, they are worth every fight. And you keep going, even when no one sees the whole picture – because you do.

NG
Mum of two girls, the oldest diagnosed with ASD

CHAPTER 1
CHOOSING TO MAINSTREAM YOUR CHILD

The decision to mainstream your child with special needs is often made with equal parts hope, determination and trepidation. It's a choice that represents not just an educational pathway, but a vision for your child's future and their place in the broader community.

When we first began contemplating our child's schooling options, I found myself awake at night weighing possibilities and imagining different futures. Would a mainstream environment overwhelm him? Would a specialist setting limit his potential? What was the 'right' choice for a child whose needs and abilities didn't fit neatly into educational categories designed for children with additional needs?

What became clear was that there is no universal right answer. The best choice depends on your unique child, your family circumstances, your available options and your values. For us, mainstreaming aligned with our hope that our child would develop alongside neurotypical peers, that he would have the same educational experiences as his younger sister would eventually have, and that he would be part of our local community.

Choosing a mainstream path doesn't mean denying your child's differences or needs. Rather, it means believing that with the right support, understanding and advocacy, the mainstream environment can adapt to accommodate and nurture your child. It means seeing the potential benefits of inclusion for both your child and their classmates, who will learn valuable lessons about diversity, empathy and different ways of experiencing the world by being in community with your child.

This chapter explores the process of making this significant decision – from understanding assessment outcomes and navigating kindergarten transitions to identifying schools that might be the right fit for your child. While the path may not always be smooth, approaching this decision with clarity and confidence creates a foundation for your child's educational journey.

A second year of kinder

If you have the option to do a second year of four-year-old kinder, I definitely suggest doing this – especially if your child is a boy. There is a lot of literature confirming another year running around in kindergarten is not going to hurt them, and that the additional time can be incredibly beneficial for special-needs children. Ask the educators, too – they will probably recommend your child doing a second year, or they might even be able to recommend a great bridging kinder. Another year of kindergarten also gives you another year of accessing early intervention support for your child. They say you never regret your child doing a second year of four-year-old kindergarten; however you might regret sending your child to school too early.

When your child is in their second year of kindergarten, ask the kinder teachers if they have any thoughts about which school might be a good next fit. Most kindergarten teachers will support you into the foundation year of primary school and can even attend the funding meeting with you at the new school (we'll talk more about this in chapter 2).

Cognitive assessments

While doing the kinder thing, you are also likely to hear about cognitive assessments. In short these are tests to work out where your child sits cognitively, and are used in many schools to determine eligibility for admission, support and everything in between.

Yep. Your child. A number on a scale.

Specialist schools use these cognitive scores as key admission criteria. They typically operate with specific cognitive ranges to ensure students are placed in environments where they will thrive.

Mainstream schools use these assessments to understand a child's cognitive profile and determine support needs.

Cognitive assessments for children with disabilities typically occur between ages three and five, before formal schooling begins. Be prepared; it's not fun.

Conducted by specialists including educational psychologists, clinical psychologists, developmental paediatricians or multidisciplinary teams, these assessments examine everything from verbal comprehension to visual-spatial skills, language development and adaptive functioning. They employ standardised tools and scales such as the Wechsler Preschool Scale, Bayley Scales, Griffiths Mental Development Scales, Developmental Assessment of Young Children, and Vineland Adaptive Behavior Scales.

The resulting scores are categorised into interpretive bands that guide educational planning and support allocation. For instance, Wechsler scale scores range from 'Extremely Low' (below 70) to 'Very Superior' (130+), while other assessments use classifications such as 'severely delayed' to 'advanced'.

These classifications translate into educational support frameworks such as Regular, Supplementary, Substantial or Extensive Support bands, which determine funding levels, classroom accommodations and eligibility for specialised programs including NDIS early intervention services and Individual Education Plans (IEPs). The interpretation of these scores is always considered alongside functional assessments, which look at how the child manages day-to-day activities and participates in various environments.

If you can survive not knowing the number, then don't find out. You don't need to know where your child sits on a scale.

Why mainstream?

Mainstreaming your special-needs child is a personal decision. You'll probably consider several factors in making the choice. We felt passionately about mainstreaming our child because:

- Our second child is neurotypical, and we wanted our children to attend the same school.
- We felt our son's speech and communication skills would develop by being around speaking children.
- We wanted our child to continue with his current speech pathologist and OT, who were able to do sessions at the mainstream school.
- We feel we live in a country where mainstream education is excellent.
- Primary schools have changed a lot since we were there (in the 80s!) and are now a lot more inclusive.

Choosing the right school

This is probably the hardest decision and one you will agonise over.

There are a lot of options out there when it comes to mainstream primary schooling. They include:

- local government primary schools
- catholic or other religious primary schools
- independent schools
- dual enrolment – a couple of days at a specialist school, a couple of days at a mainstream school.

My advice for what to do during the decision-making process:

- **Go on tours.** Get a list together of the schools you want to visit. Start watching for open days or open mornings. Walk around the school. Hear what they present and what they say. See who does all the talking. See how you and your child feel in that environment. Often you'll instinctively know if the school is for you.

- **Make sure the school prioritises inclusion of children with disabilities.** You can tell easily how inclusive a school is by talking to them. Do they have staff to support students with special needs? Do they have other special-needs students enrolled already?

- **Check the Australian Curriculum, Assessment and Reporting Authority (ACARA) website to find out about school sizes.** We sought out a small-sized school. We didn't want our child to get lost or not get enough attention in a big school.

- **Study the scene.** Find out more about the school by going to their school fete or any open school events. Ask your networks about the school. Talk to your allied health professionals – they visit lots of schools and know the ones that make it work. You want to ensure the school is a good fit for the whole family.

- **Consider travel and logistics.** This could be a seven-year commitment to drop-offs and pick-ups. Will this option work for the long term?

If there is a school you like and think will work for you and your family, approach the school. In Australia, you are zoned for a local mainstream primary school; however, your child can attend a different school if the one they are zoned for isn't suitable for them or your family's needs. You will need to appeal to the principal at your chosen school in plenty of time, and it is ultimately their decision whether to accept your child's enrolment. Ask for an application and write a letter to the principal explaining why your child should be at the school. Explain your situation, and what you as a family would bring to the school – not only diverse perspectives but a commitment to help, support and volunteer. Follow up with a phone call, or ask for a meeting to discuss further.

Most schools will also tell you if they think you are the right fit for them. If they don't feel they are the best choice for your child, it will hurt hearing this; but it is for the best that you know this. It's not personal. It is about whether the school has the right resources, attitude, teachers and so on to make support for your child a reality. Some schools are set up better to provide support and the right environment for special-needs children.

The better the fit, the better everything will go, so take your time visiting and visualising what is going to be a good fit for everyone involved.

PRINCIPAL INSIGHT

At the point of enrolment, I listen to parents' hopes and dreams for their child who has significant learning needs. I stress to the parents that I will only commit to a level of support that I know I can provide in terms of physical resources and additional personnel. As I have become more experienced, I am more realistic about what my school can provide. Sometimes this is enough for parents, while on other occasions they prefer other options for their child.

There was a family who had four children on the autism spectrum. The parents wished to enrol all their children at my school. When I considered what each child needed, I was conscious of the impact on the teachers: new challenges, additional meetings, more training and possibly more stress. I was also conscious that each child would require more from the teachers, hence taking time away from the other students. Could I meet all the needs of all four of these children? I wasn't confident that I could. I offered a place to two of the children, not the other two siblings. Wanting all the children to be together, the family withdrew their application.

Andrew Oberthur
Catholic primary school principal
Extract from his book, Are You Ready for School?

Advocating for your child

Advocating for a special-needs child in the Australian education system requires a combination of persistence, knowledge and a little bit of strategy.

Building collaborative relationships while maintaining firm boundaries is a great place to start. Work to develop positive connections with teachers, therapists, learning support and the school leadership. Don't hesitate to respectfully challenge decisions that don't serve your child's needs. Learn to balance being assertive and being constructive. Phrases such as,

'How can we work together on this?' or, 'What strategies would you recommend we try for this situation?' often yield better results than confrontational approaches.

Managing a child with a disability at a mainstream school requires clear and persistent advocacy. The school won't automatically know what your child needs – you have to ask.

I have adopted a mindset of 'always ask' when it comes to my child's education. They might say no, but if they say yes, it's a win that directly benefits him. I've requested accommodations for school swimming carnivals, additional support during excursions and flexibility with certain school policies such as uniforms. I approach these conversations with specific goals in mind and a collaborative attitude.

Remember that you are the expert on your child, and your voice is essential.

THE DIFFICULT PARENT

I am sitting in a meeting. Around the table is a team of fellow professionals: physios, speech therapists, OTs and psychologists. They have been talking about a parent of a young woman with learning disabilities. The parent has just been described as 'difficult', 'over-attached', 'unable to let go' and 'interfering'. I hear these words and I take no action.

Two decades on, I am sitting in a workshop. Around the table are fellow parents of children with additional needs. No longer part of the professional team, I am now a member of the parental team. Several of these parents have described themselves, confidently, as 'difficult parents'. And this sets me thinking – if we peel off the label, who might the person behind it actually be? Who is the 'difficult parent' of a child with additional needs?

A parent who is fully in touch with the weight of their responsibility towards their child.

A parent who knows that they are, and probably always will be, their child's advocate and ambassador in the world.

A parent who wakes up in the middle of the night thinking: What will happen to my child when I'm dead? Will they be safe and happy? Will someone abuse or take advantage of them? What will happen if they can't look after themselves?

A parent who may well, like myself and my husband, have been told that their child's prognosis will depend on how committed they are as parents, and how determined they are to practise therapeutic recommendations and provide requisite support.

A parent who had not necessarily expected to be leading this life. They may have assumed, like most parents, that they would be taking their child to Scouts, football practice, ballet or playdates with friends. In reality, they are taking them to appointments with neurologists, paediatricians, OTs and physios; they are preparing them for operations and MRI scans.

Most people want to be liked. But the difficult parent is willing to take the risk of not being liked because their child needs them to, however uncomfortable that makes them feel. If they make a suggestion, check something out or follow something up, they are not trying to undermine professionals. They are trying to ensure that their child gets what they need. Sometimes they notice things that other people don't.

Most hate to intervene at any level. The worry about how to approach a professional may keep us away at night. We do not raise issues lightly and there is no handbook. We have to learn from our mistakes. This sometimes upsets professionals and makes them dislike us. A parent may have experienced painful encounters with professionals – medical or educational or from social services – in the past and may be carrying the memory of these nightmare encounters like a tortoise carries its shell.

In theory, a professional can shut the door at the end of the day and get on with their life. A parent of a child with additional needs can't do that. They are on call 24 hours a day for the rest of their lives.

A difficult parent may be grieving the life they expected their child, and their family, to lead. A difficult parent may not have slept much in many years. A difficult parent may be determined that their child will live the richest, fullest possible life and be encouraged to show the world who they really are.

If that's the sort of parent I have to be, then so be it. Had I known this two decades ago, I would have stood up in that meeting and defended that 'difficult parent'. Now, I understand.

By Judith Hooper
Reproduced courtesy of SEN Magazine

Being organised and maintaining clear documentation is a powerful tool when advocating for your child. Create a well-structured electronic filing system that keeps your child's important documents accessible. Keep a calendar of all appointments, school events, review dates and deadlines. Maintain contact lists for all your child's support members, too – there needs to be someone who has all the details always. Some parents also find it valuable to keep a running document of questions or concerns, rather than trying to remember everything during appointments. I was once told to get one book and keep everything in there. This is very handy as it ensures you remember everything from meeting to meeting. This level of organisation might seem overwhelming at first, but it dramatically strengthens your ability to advocate effectively. When you can quickly access relevant information or provide specific examples to support your requests, you position yourself as a well-prepared and knowledgeable advocate for your child's needs.

Understanding your child's rights and the education system's obligations is essential, and I will go through this in more detail in the next chapter. All knowledge helps you advocate from a position of strength and allows you to understand what adjustments or supports your child is entitled to receive while at school.

Finally, finding the right support network strengthens your advocacy. Connect with other parents who are having a similar experience. Also have some people who are outside your bubble. Having someone you can bounce ideas off and have a cry to does help.

Remember that advocacy is a marathon, not a sprint. Pick your battles wisely and maintain energy for long-term advocacy. Sometimes small wins build to bigger changes. Some days feel like a loss and really hurt – you and your child.

This is the journey, isn't it?

Chapter summary

- Doing an extra year of kindergarten lets your child grow at their own pace, while giving you more time to access those vital early supports.

- Take your time exploring different schools. Check out their grounds, chat with staff and get a feel for how welcoming they are to all kids. Trust your gut when you walk in – you will know if it feels right.

- Whether mainstream schooling is right for your family often comes down to keeping siblings together and giving your child plenty of chances to learn alongside their peers.

- Be organised with your paperwork and build good relationships with school staff.

- Find your support crew, both within and outside the school community.

- Know your rights and pick your battles wisely – it's a long journey ahead.

CHAPTER 2
KNOWING YOUR RIGHTS

One of the most powerful tools you'll need on your mainstreaming journey isn't found in a therapy session or classroom – it's knowledge. Understanding your child's rights and the obligations of schools and education systems provides the foundation for effective advocacy and informed decision-making.

When my child started his primary-school journey, I quickly realised how crucial it was to understand the legal frameworks, funding mechanisms and support structures available to us. Like many parents, I initially felt overwhelmed by the complexity of these systems. Terms such as 'reasonable adjustments', 'NCCD funding' and 'Individual Education Plans' seemed like a foreign language. Yet, as I learned to navigate these systems, I found that knowledge truly is power.

What I've discovered is that while Australian legislation provides strong protections for children with disabilities, effectively accessing these rights often requires parents to be informed, persistent and strategic. Schools generally want to do the right thing, but they operate within systems with limited resources and competing priorities. When you understand both your child's entitlements and the constraints schools face, you can work more effectively within these realities to secure appropriate support.

This knowledge doesn't just help you advocate for better support – it changes the dynamic of your interactions with the education system. Rather than approaching meetings from a position of uncertainty, you can engage as an informed partner in your child's education. You'll know when to push for more and when the school is genuinely doing all it can within the parameters it's facing.

This chapter explores the legislative frameworks that protect your child's right to education, how school funding for students with disabilities works, what reasonable adjustments look like in practice, and how to navigate the system when things aren't working as they should.

Inclusion in schools

Primary schools' approach to inclusion has evolved significantly since the mid-1980s when I went to school. What was once considered revolutionary – mainstreaming students with different needs – has become a fundamental aspect of educational philosophy.

Traditional school structures weren't originally designed with neurodiverse children or those with additional needs in mind – often leaving these students feeling like square pegs trying to fit into round holes. Yet schools are increasingly recognising this mismatch and adapting their approaches.

Government funding has transformed the physical infrastructure of schools with accessibility ramps, lifts and modified toilets, while also supporting specialised intervention programs for students who need additional support. Today's schools often feature sensory rooms, quiet zones and specialised equipment to accommodate diverse learning needs.

However, true inclusion goes beyond physical accommodations. It requires a mindset shift among educators, school staff and students – creating a culture where diversity is celebrated rather than merely tolerated. The most successful inclusive environments combine thoughtful design with educators who genuinely believe in every child's right to equal educational opportunities, regardless of physical, cognitive or social differences. While there's still progress to be made, many schools are reimagining their environments and teaching methods to better embrace all types of learners and their unique contributions to the school community.

STUDENT INSIGHT

I've had peers with special needs in my class for as long as I can remember. It's fun and interesting to be around people who are different from me. Having classmates with diverse abilities has helped me learn to communicate and work with others in different ways – ways I might never have learned otherwise.

I love helping others, and when there are children with additional needs in my class, I sometimes get to work with them and help them. I've learned that people with special needs can be really good at lots of things, like spelling or climbing trees, for example. That means we can both learn from each other.

It's good that everyone is included at school. We all get to be friends and try things in new ways together. That makes our class a nice place to be.

Dottie
Year 4 student

PARENT INSIGHT

As a parent, I truly value that my child shares a classroom with children who have special needs. The world is diverse, and I believe the classroom should reflect that. It's important that children learn from a young age that we are not all the same – but that everyone should be included and respected.

Being in class with children who are different helps build empathy, patience and understanding. These are life skills that can't be taught from a book but come from real-life experience. When children grow up learning side-by-side with others of all abilities, they are less likely to discriminate and more likely to stand up for inclusion and fairness.

I believe every child has the right to an education at the school of their family's choice. Inclusion isn't just a principle – it's a right. What I've seen is that having children with special needs in class isn't just good for the special-needs children; it's good for *all* the children. It gives other students the chance to learn how to help, how to connect, and how to see the value in everyone.

Watching my daughter form friendships with classmates who may experience the world differently is incredibly heartwarming. Seeing her make sure others are included and treated kindly reminds me what truly matters. The diversity in friendships that grow in inclusive classrooms is beautiful.

Practically speaking, when there are aides or support staff in the classroom, it benefits everyone. The teacher has more help and students have more support, which creates a better learning environment for the whole class.

Inclusion makes classrooms stronger, kinder and more prepared for the real world – and I'm so grateful my child gets to be part of that.

Frances Murphy
Mother of Dottie

Children's rights

In Australia, education is considered a fundamental right for all children.

Education is compulsory for all children aged between six and 16 years old (Year 1 to Year 10), though specific age requirements can vary between states and territories.

All children in Australia have the right to free education at government (public) schools. This includes:

- Primary education (typically Years F to 6)
- Secondary education (typically Years 7 to 12)
- Access to qualified teachers and basic educational resources
- Standard curriculum delivery.

Furthermore:

- Children with disabilities have the right to reasonable adjustments and support to access education.
- Indigenous students must have access to the additional support programs available.
- Children in remote areas must have access to distance education options.
- Non-English speaking students have the right to English language support.

While public education is a right, Australian families can also choose to:

- send children to private/independent schools (at their own cost)
- homeschool (following state/territory requirements)
- access the Catholic education system.

Disability rights

Understanding your rights when mainstreaming your child with special needs is fundamental to ensuring they receive appropriate education. Your child has the legal right to attend their local mainstream school, and that school must make reasonable adjustments to accommodate their needs. As a parent, you have the right to be actively involved in all decisions about your child's education, from planning support services to reviewing progress.

While mainstream schooling is a right, you retain the choice between mainstream and specialist education settings based on your child's specific needs and circumstances. It's important to know you can request meetings with school staff at any time to discuss concerns or review arrangements, and the school must engage in meaningful consultation about adjustments and support.

These rights are protected under the Disability Standards for Education and various state policies. They aim to ensure your child has access to quality education in an inclusive environment. You also have the right to appeal decisions and seek advocacy support if you feel your child's needs aren't being adequately met.

State and territory programs

Each state and territory education department has its own programs that operate for students with disabilities. Broadly, these include:

Funding support mechanisms

- Individual student funding based on assessed needs
- School-based funding for support programs
- Funding for specialised equipment
- Supplementary funding for high-needs students
- Transport and mobility assistance funding

Assessment and identification
- Standardised disability assessment processes
- Regular reviews of student needs
- Professional specialist assessments
- Support with documentation requirements
- Consultation with health professionals

Support staff and services
- Special education teachers
- Teacher aides/learning support officers
- Allied health professionals (speech therapy, OT, physiotherapy, psychology)
- Visiting specialist teachers
- School-based support teams
- Regional support coordinators

Education adjustments
- Individual Education Plans (IEPs)
- Modified curriculum delivery
- Adjusted assessment methods
- Specialised resources and equipment
- Physical environment modifications
- Technology and communication aids

Professional development
- Teacher training in inclusive practices
- Specialist skills development for teachers

- Regular learning about best practices and the latest research
- Collaboration with disability experts
- Support staff training

Program models
- Mainstream class support
- Special education units/classes
- Specialist schools
- Combined delivery options
- Distance education support
- Hospital school services

Coordination and management
- School-based coordination
- Regional support networks
- Multi-agency collaboration
- Family partnerships approaches
- Regular review processes
- Case management services

Support services
- Transport assistance
- Equipment loans
- Technology support
- Therapy services
- Transition support
- Before/after-school support

Disability inclusion school funding

As a parent of a special-needs child you'll hear all about funding. But what does it actually mean?

In short, school funding for special-needs students is funding provided by the government to the school to enable targeted support for each child in need. It is primarily administered via the Nationally Consistent Collection of Data (NCCD), which schools use to identify students needing additional support. This is a different funding pool from the NDIS. Not all students with special needs will receive school funding, even if they are eligible for NDIS funding. The school will normally be able to tell you whether they think funding is needed or accessible for your child, and will discuss the process with you.

Let's take a look at what the process typically involves.

Initial assessment and evidence gathering

The school collects evidence of your child's needs, including professional reports, previous school records or kindergarten records, and observations of how your child functions. They document adjustments already being made and their effectiveness. The school will seek input from its educators, your child's kindergarten educators and any external professionals working with your child.

Consultation process

The primary consultation opportunity is the funding meeting. This meeting will be set and run by your state/territory's department of education. You will have an opportunity to briefly speak to your child's strengths, then you and the school will run through your child's needs, current supports and proposed adjustments. This is usually a long list, and it's important to be prepared to discuss every detail and provide examples and stories. The school will explain how they plan to support your child and how the funding will be used. This will also involve developing or presenting the IEP or similar document.

Ultimately what you are discussing in detail is the adjustments and accommodations that are needed for your child to access school.

School **adjustments** are the bigger changes schools make to teaching, learning and assessment that help kids with additional needs access the curriculum and join in like everyone else. These can be pretty major modifications to how teaching normally works and might include different teaching methods, changing what is taught or using special support staff. In Australia, adjustments are officially recognised under the Disability Standards for Education. You will discuss in detail a number adjustments that will be needed to support your child.

School **accommodations** are the specific, practical tweaks that help with particular barriers without completely changing educational standards. They might include extra time for tests, using a wobble chair, providing materials in different formats or making physical changes to the classroom. While people often use 'accommodations' and 'adjustments' to mean the same thing, 'reasonable adjustments' is the official term that covers both smaller accommodations and bigger adjustments.

The level of adjustment your child requires is determined in the funding meeting – on a scale from 'support provided within quality differentiated teaching practice' through to 'extensive adjustment'. Each decision affects funding levels and is based on the collected evidence and consultation with the school and you.

This meeting is intense and can take anywhere between two and three hours. My advice is to avoid work and other activities before and after the meeting if possible, to give yourself space to prepare and process. Fun times.

Implementation and review

Within six weeks of submitting all the paperwork, the school should advise you about the funding decision. Funding is back paid to when the school started providing support, so you won't miss out even if it took a while for your funding review to happen. The school will decide how the funding is allocated, and the school should communicate to you how the support will be delivered. This may include learning support aide time, specialised resources and equipment, professional development for staff and so on. Reviews are set up in the funding meeting to ensure the support remains appropriate.

It is important to remember that this process takes time, especially if new assessments are needed. Also, schools receive your child's funding as part of their overall budget and have discretion in how it's used. However, you have a right to be involved in discussions about how support is provided to your child.

It's important to understand what a school receiving a child's funding actually means in practice. While funding is valuable, it doesn't automatically translate to one-on-one aide support for your child for the entire school day (and the funding is never enough to cover this). Instead, it might mean your child receives targeted intervention sessions, specialised learning programs or shared in-class support. Today's classrooms often have multiple students with additional needs, so support staff typically work with several students, rotating their attention based on individual requirements and learning goals.

While support in any form is valuable and helps students access their learning, it's essential to remember that a key goal of additional support is to build independence. As children grow older, most naturally seek more autonomy in their school life. The aim is to help students develop the skills and strategies they need to manage their learning more independently. Schools work to find the right balance – providing the necessary support while gradually building students' confidence and ability to tackle challenges on their own. This approach helps prepare students for their future learning journey and life beyond school.

PARENT INSIGHT

Having worked in early childhood education for many years I believed I had quite a strong grasp of educational funding and how to be a strong advocate for children. And I did … to a point. However, having my own child diagnosed with additional needs in primary school, I found myself navigating a whole new world of funding, adjustments and getting the best support. Very quickly I realised that I needed to re-educate myself and gain a deeper understanding of my rights and the rights of my child.

As a parent I have the right to be involved in discussions and decisions about my child. I have the right to ask questions, have documentation shared, be communicated with effectively, and have teachers and school leaders listen to my perspective, and my child's perspective. My child has the right to a high-quality, inclusive learning environment which means I have the right to ask for adaptations in order for my child's needs to be met. I have the right to ask the hard and uncomfortable questions so our family and the school can work together to ensure the best outcomes for my child.

I understand that there will always be funding limitations and systemic barriers, but persistence and knowledge are powerful tools. When I know my rights, I am not only a better parent but also a better educator as I try to advocate for all children.

Tarryn Holland
Mum of two girls, one with additional needs

Complaints process

The funding process is a government process therefore there are very clear processes for registering complaints or issues. It is always good to know the process if something goes wrong. Here's how it works:

Level 1 – School-based resolution

- Discuss your issue with your classroom teacher and learning support team.
- Request a formal meeting with the school principal.
- Document all conversations and keep copies of emails/letters.
- Allow a reasonable time (typically two to four weeks) for a response.
- Request written confirmation of agreed actions.

Level 2 – Education department

- Contact your state/territory education department.
- Submit a formal written complaint.
- Request advocacy support if needed.
- Check the timelines in which your department must investigate.
- Keep records of all correspondence.

Level 3 – External bodies

- The Australian Human Rights Commission for discrimination cases.
- Your state/territory anti-discrimination board.
- The Commonwealth Ombudsman for government school issues.
- Your state/territory independent school ombudsman for independent school issues.

I have included some key contacts for you to have on hand at the end of this book. Please check the appropriate websites for the most up-to-date contacts and process information.

Chapter summary

- Knowing your rights matters. All Australian children have the right to an education, and schools must make reasonable adjustments for those with additional needs.

- The NCCD funding process takes time but helps the school support your child. Prepare for an intense funding meeting and give yourself the whole day off if you possibly can.

- Each state runs its support programs differently, but they all cover the basics: funding, assessments, support staff and learning adjustments.

- Get your paperwork sorted early – schools need evidence of your child's needs from professional reports and previous records to access support.

- If there are issues, there's a path to follow – start with your teacher, then principal, and know you can take it higher if needed.

CHAPTER 3

STARTING SCHOOL

The first day of school is a milestone that looms large in every parent's mind. For parents of children with additional needs, this transition can feel particularly momentous – filled with both hope and apprehension. Will the teachers understand my child? How will my child cope with the new routines and expectations? Will they make friends? Will they be supported properly?

When my child started school, I remember standing at the school gate with a knot in my stomach that felt like it might never unravel. We had prepared extensively – visits to the school, meetings with teachers, social stories, practising with the uniform – yet I still wondered if we had done enough. Would our carefully constructed supports hold up in this new environment?

The reality is that school transition doesn't happen in a single day or week. It's an ongoing process that unfolds over months and even years. It's about building relationships, establishing routines, navigating new social landscapes and creating systems that support your child's unique way of learning and being in the world.

This chapter explores how to navigate this significant transition, from the practical preparations before day one to managing the everyday realities of school life. While the journey may not always be smooth, with the right approach and supports, mainstream schooling can offer rich opportunities for growth, learning and connection for your child.

Trust and collaboration

Your child's success at school is determined by the quality of the relationship between you and their teacher, and that journey starts even before your child's first day of school.

As Andrew Oberthur explains in his book, *Are You Ready for School?*, the most important people in a child's life are their parents and their teacher – since they spend most of their waking hours with these people. He explains that the key to a child's successful educational journey is having a parent-teacher relationship built around a culture of trust, collaboration and enquiry.

Parents need to trust the teachers and the school to provide high-quality education in a safe environment. In short, teachers stand *in loco parentis* (in place of a parent).

Oberthur quotes Hendersen and Berla (1994) and explains:

> *The most accurate predictor of a student's achievement in school is not income or social status but the extent to which that student's family is able to create a home environment*

that encourages learning; express high (but not unrealistic) expectations for their children's achievement and future careers; and, become involved in their children's education at school and in the community.

Having a child with additional needs or a disability means you are going to have to trust the teachers and school, and get involved and informed. Read the newsletters, attend the parent-teacher meetings, do the funding reviews, sign all the paperwork. You need to be heavily involved in your child's education even before day one.

Foundation transition

The transition process starts the moment you find out where your child will be attending school. Every time you mention the school's name to your family or talk about how your child will be going to school, you are engaging in the transition process.

Before my child started school, I consumed all the content I could about starting school. I found numerous books for neurotypical kids and a bit of specialist literature and webinars from the disability associations. There is heaps of good information and checklists out there already.

The school transition days are great, but they happen in November, and it is a long time between then and when the school year starts in early February.

Some of the things that helped us:

- Getting our child's school uniform early and trying it out, including him wearing it on transition days. Cutting off the labels and prewashing everything. Labelling every item with our child's name. Focusing on supporting our child to try on and try out everything. We wanted to develop as much routine as possible early on.

- The primary school teacher who was going to be teaching our son's class visited both of his kindergartens and met his current educators. She observed our son before he started school, and also chatted to his kinder teachers, so she knew what to expect. The more information the school has on your child, the better the transition will be. If the school doesn't suggest this for your child, ask for it. I did take the approach of eyes wide open. The more information the school had about our child, including his interests, his strengths and his needs, the more they did to support us.

- Getting pictures of the school, teacher/s, aides and staff and explaining all of this to our child in a social story (more on this in the next section). The more pictures you have of the child's school experience – their classroom, friends, where to line up and so on – the easier the transition will go. We create a social story before the end of each year of schooling to prepare our child for the transition to summer holidays and then the return to school. We continually update the social story before school returns as we have more details such as the class he will be in, his teacher and which of his friends will be in that class.

- Visiting the school on the weekend before school returns. This gives our son a chance to play in the playgrounds and check out all the little differences at the school from the year before, without the pressure of other people being present. The buildings are not open, but being on school grounds allows our son to start getting comfortable in the space again.

- Visiting our classroom teacher the day before school returns. This only takes ten minutes but makes a huge difference to the year. We get an opportunity to see the classroom quietly and reconnect with the teacher after the long summer holidays. This also allows me to give the teacher a quick update on how the holidays were and where my child is at.
- Getting to know the rules and helping our child to understand them. There are lots of rules at school. Some of them will make sense to your child but others won't. Schools also have a lot of implicit or informal rules, which our children sometimes miss. Help your child work these out so they know the lay of the land at school.

Over the years I have learned to clearly ask for things we need – for example, the ten-minute visit with the teacher the day before school starts, speech therapy starting as soon as possible and so on. I ask in advance and follow up, as people are human and do forget. These small things make a huge difference in the transition each year, so we prioritise them.

Learning new rules and routines

School is full of new routines. There is more to learn than you think. By the time our children even get into the classroom each morning they have had to follow hundreds of little rules.

Consider the tasks our children must complete and rules they need to follow between the car and the classroom each morning:

- Get out of car.
- Put on backpack.
- Line up for the crossing, but don't press the button – the crossing supervisor has to do that.

- Say good morning to the crossing supervisor.
- Walk on the left side of the path.
- Let bigger kids and those riding bikes and scooters pass on the right.
- Put backpack down in one place during summer months and a different place during winter months.
- Say good morning to the teacher.
- Say hello to friends.
- Listen out for the bell.
- Line up with the class.
- Enter the classroom via a specific route.

What a test of their executive functioning skills before they even get to the classroom!

Some of these routines and rules play to a child's advantage, while others are very hard for children to follow.

Rules and routines also change. Just when you think you have one down pat, the season changes and the rules change again.

We find one of the best ways to impart the school rules and routines is via social stories. The more personalised, the better.

Social stories are short, personalised narratives created for children with additional needs, especially those with autism or developmental delays. They use clear, straightforward language to show and explain social situations, expected behaviours and experiences. These help children understand and feel prepared for situations and scenarios they might face. By breaking down social rules and expectations into bite-sized pieces of information, social stories help reduce worry, build confidence and develop important social skills. These stories work best when they include pictures or visual supports that show children exactly what to expect in different situations. We have created social stories for a variety of things: keeping with the group, toileting at school, keeping shoes and clothes on, moving up a grade, athletics day, mid-year change of teacher, illness, pregnancies, new therapists, swimming lessons, the school production, school excursions and more.

The more these activities are repeated the better our child gets at them and the more photos we can use for the social story next time.

All these rules and routines impact our child, though, and there is a build-up over time. By the end of the school day our little one is done. By the end of the school term, again he is done. By the end of the year, oh my, we are all done.

He is over people telling him what to do. The noise. The rules. He is done.

PARENT INSIGHT

My journey into social stories began with my four-year-old – an adventurous little boy who would ride his bike down stairs, yet struggled with every preschool drop-off.

With school looming, I knew I needed to find a way to help him feel confident and ready. A slow transition with me staying in the room until he felt comfortable wasn't going to be an option. I just wanted him to be one of those kids who hugged their parents goodbye and went into their classroom bubbling with excitement.

I started researching strategies for anxiety management and separation anxiety in young kids and consulted with the experts, which led me to discover social stories. These are short, personalised stories that explain a new event, introduce a new person or reflect on an experience. They were originally developed for autistic children but can be effective for any child facing change.

The idea of explaining what would happen and building familiarity through stories and pictures seemed sensible, and I began writing stories for my son to prepare him for school: what would be the same as preschool, what would be different, who his teachers would be and what would happen at drop-off. I included photos of his school, the principal and his teacher.

The result? On his first day he came up to me and whispered, 'You can go now, Mum.'

I now make stories to prepare him and his younger brother for milestones big and small. While they may still feel apprehensive, they also have the understanding and confidence needed to have a go.

I wanted to share this approach with other families, particularly those with anxious, autistic or highly sensitive children, which ultimately inspired the app, Courageous Kids.

Dr Kathryn Hackman
Mum of two boys
Founder of Courageous Kids App

Cognitive load

Cognitive load theory, developed by John Sweller, helps us understand how children process information in the classroom. The theory explains that our working memory has a limited capacity, typically holding only four to seven pieces of information at once. Students with learning difficulties can often hold fewer pieces of information, or process things more slowly. This means they are starting with less available cognitive space before even beginning to tackle learning tasks.

For students with learning difficulties, their cognitive load is frequently at capacity due to the extra mental effort required for tasks that other students might find automatic. For example, a student with dyslexia uses significant cognitive resources just to decode text, leaving less capacity for comprehending the meaning, while a child with ADHD may use considerable mental energy filtering out classroom distractions, reducing their available resources for learning new content.

This understanding helps explain why our children often experience fatigue more quickly, may struggle with multi-step instructions or find it challenging to engage with complex learning tasks. They reach their cognitive load threshold more quickly due to their additional processing demands.

When starting school, cognitive load is intensified as children must simultaneously process unfamiliar routines, new social dynamics, different expectations and learning. For children with learning difficulties, this transition period requires significantly more time and support, as their already taxed cognitive resources are further stretched by the sheer volume of new information. As the years go by we have seen this again and again for our child at the start of each new year and at the end of each term. Recognising this heightened cognitive demand is essential for creating supportive transitions that allow all children, especially those with additional needs, to adjust to school life.

Time to adjust

Starting school takes time for our children. Time to settle in. Time to learn the routines and understand the rules. Time to learn names and faces. Time to process all the new things. Foundation is hard. There's so much to learn every day, and so many new experiences.

We did very little on the rest day during Term 1, choosing to spend quiet time at home. But the term went fast and before we knew it, the school week shifted to five days.

Keep in mind that your child might not be able to do the full five days, and that's okay. You can choose to pick them up early any day you want, or when you think they need it. Don't feel bad about doing this. This is not forever, and these sorts of arrangements can change term to term depending on your child. They will need time to settle in. It might even take a year.

Everything takes time within a school, too. It takes a lot of time (and emails) to start speech pathology and OT. It takes time to sort out issues. It takes time for things to resolve.

As we navigate school routines, it's worth considering different frameworks for understanding time itself. The concept of 'crip time' from disability studies offers valuable perspective here. It acknowledges that disabled people experience time differently.

For our children, this might mean recognising that development follows its own timeline, not the standardised schedules of traditional schooling.

Embracing crip time means valuing your child's unique pace and understanding that their timeline for adapting to school life deserves respect and accommodation. It's not about 'falling behind' but about honouring each child's individual journey.

Sickness

I cannot talk about the first year of school (or any year of school, actually) without discussing sickness.

Get ready for it. We have had everything: lice; gastro; Covid; respiratory syncytial virus; school sores (impetigo); whooping cough.

Not only do our children, who sometimes have complex health needs, seem to catch everything, so do we as parents. School contains so many new germs. All I can suggest is couch and doona days with the iPad for the children.

In good news, the amount of sickness does lessen over the years once your child has already caught most of the bugs going around.

We find Term 3 particularly hard every year. The shine of the start of the year has gone. It is germ central in every classroom. It is cold and everyone is tired. So, I sometimes pick up my child at lunchtime on a Friday. It took me a good couple of years for a classroom teacher to say to me I can just pick him up when I want, and I don't have to feel bad about it. Once she had given me permission I felt much better doing it.

Toileting

Yes, I am going there.

Many children with disabilities are not independent at toileting by the time they get to school. No matter what we tried, we weren't ready. It was hard and embarrassing for my child and us, however it is a fact of parenting children with additional needs.

Don't be embarrassed.

Schools have a duty of care to support students with disabilities in their toileting needs, but this must be properly planned, documented and carried out by appropriately trained staff. While teachers cannot provide intimate personal care such as wiping, schools typically employ Student Learning Support Officers (SLSOs) or teacher's aides who have specific training in personal care support. These staff members must have appropriate qualifications and Working with Children Checks in place. Two trained staff must be present for intimate care tasks. All care provided must be documented and specific times are usually scheduled for toileting support, along with procedures for unscheduled needs.

The school should work with the family and OT to create a detailed personal care plan that outlines the student's needs, required support and specific procedures, while respecting the student's dignity and independence. The personal care plan should document practical considerations and how to promote independence where possible. For children who need toileting support (such as help with buttons, or supervision) but not intimate care, different procedures might apply – but these still need to be clearly documented and carried out by appropriate staff.

While some schools might ask parents to provide intimate care themselves if trained staff aren't available, this isn't a long-term solution – and there is a chance your child will be at that school for seven years. Keep working on it, as both the school and you need your child to work towards independence in these skills.

Don't forget: schools have an obligation under disability legislation to provide appropriate support and reasonable adjustments for students with disabilities, including personal care needs.

Chapter summary

- Starting school is all about trust. Building solid relationships with teachers and getting involved right from the start sets everyone up for success.

- Give transition plenty of time. Start months before school begins with social stories, uniforms and quiet visits to get familiar with the space.

- Children with additional needs have a huge amount to process each day – even just following the morning routine from car to class takes heaps of mental energy. Expect them to be exhausted at the end of each day.

- School germs are real. Be ready for lots of sick days in that first year and don't feel bad about early pick-ups when it all gets too much.

- Supporting children with toileting and personal care requires careful planning. Work with the school to sort out a solid plan that works for everyone.

CHAPTER 4
GOALS

When you have a child with additional needs, the concept of goals takes on a whole new meaning. The traditional milestones that many parents take for granted – walking by one, talking by two, reading by six – often need to be reimagined, stretched or completely redefined.

For our child, our goals have always been both simpler and more complex than those set for neurotypical children. The first time he typed on his device to communicate was as meaningful to us as another child's first word might be to their parents. Each small skill mastered represents countless hours of practice, support and persistence – from both our child and everyone working with him.

What I have learned over the years is that goals for children with additional needs require a delicate balance. They need to be ambitious enough to inspire progress yet realistic enough to prevent burnout and frustration. They need to encompass not just academic achievements but also life skills, social development and emotional wellbeing. And, perhaps most importantly, they need to be flexible, adapting to your child's unique journey rather than forcing your child to adapt to predetermined expectations.

This chapter explores how to set, track and celebrate goals that truly serve your child's development. I look at how to coordinate goals across various support professionals, how the school's Individual Education Plan (IEP) fits into your broader vision, and how to maintain perspective when progress doesn't follow a straight line.

Short-term and long-term goals

Having goals is very important. It allows us to have something to work towards, collaborate on and measure against. Goals change and develop over time. Sometimes they need to be broken down into numerous small goals leading to a bigger goal.

We've all been taught about SMART goals (specific, measured, achievable, realistic and timely) but these don't always work for families of special-needs children. As much as you might want to put a time limit on achieving a goal, this will often just lead to disappointment. As much as you might want to measure progress, this may be hard to do.

We are constantly revising our short-term and long-term goals for our child. We have been working on some of our goals for years.

Some of our long-term goals include:

- Finish Year 6 at our current primary school.
- Complete toileting independence. (We have been toilet training for the past six years, since he was three years old. He's made huge leaps forward and gained a lot of independence, but this goal has a lot of little parts to it too.)
- To be reading at the end of Year 3.
- Ability to express sickness and emotions.

Some of our recent short-term goals have included:

- Transition to new teacher and new classroom location next school year.
- Ensure new speech pathologist is up and running (and weekly) in Term 1.
- Get a sense of the new things our child will experience this year so we can start preparing.
- Integrate his Augmentative and Alternative Communication (AAC) device and its use into the classroom.

On top of this, we have separate goals with:

- The school
- The speech pathologist
- The OT
- The psychologist
- Other health professionals.

So many goals. One little person.

Individual Education Plans

Thank you to Cleo Westhorpe, Founder of the Inclusive School, for contributing this content.

Many of your school-related goals will culminate in the creation of an Individual Education Plan/Program (IEP) for your child.

An IEP is a legally binding document designed to ensure that students with disabilities receive the support they need to access and thrive in their education. These plans are essential tools for personalising learning and ensuring that every student has the opportunity to achieve to their full potential.

Key components of an IEP

IEPs are mandatory for students with disabilities and must include:

- **Current level of functioning and needs:** A detailed description of the student's strengths, challenges and areas requiring support.
- **Short- and long-term learning goals:** Clearly defined goals that guide 'the team' towards the student's progress and achievement.
- **Specific strategies and adjustments:** Strategies, adjustments and modifications that support your child to access and thrive in their learning.
- **Regular review dates:** This generally comes in the form of Student Support Group (SSG) meetings. Typically these are held once per term, but this can vary between schools. These are scheduled opportunities to assess progress and make necessary adjustments to the IEP. IEPs are generally updated annually to reflect the academic calendar, unless

new information comes to light or a particular strength or challenge emerges.
- **Input from all stakeholders:** Collaboration between teachers, parents, specialists and other allied health and support staff will go a long way to developing a comprehensive and effective plan.

Implementation of IEPs in schools

Schools and teachers implement IEPs as living documents that guide their daily practice and planning. When designing lessons, teachers incorporate required adjustments and modifications to ensure that each student's individual needs are met while maintaining overall class momentum. Examples of adjustments may include:

- Extended time on assessments for students with processing difficulties.
- Alternative formats for instructional materials, such as audiobooks or enlarged print.
- Assistive technology, such as speech-to-text software or communication devices.
- Behaviour support plans to help students navigate social and emotional challenges in the classroom and/or playground.

Collaboration between educators and specialists

Regular collaboration should occur between classroom teachers and support staff, such as literacy intervention specialists, speech therapists, OTs and school psychologists and counsellors. These professionals should work together to plan programs and interventions based on the IEP. Schools may also facilitate meetings with parents and caregivers to ensure their input is reflected in the student's learning plan. At the very minimum, parents and guardians must be aware of an IEP and have provided input and given their approval of the plan.

Progress monitoring and adjustments

Progress monitoring is an absolutely crucial aspect of IEP implementation. Teachers should continually document student achievements and challenges against IEP goals through observations, assessments and student self-reflections. This ongoing assessment enables educators to:

- Make timely adjustments to teaching methods, materials and approaches
- Identify new strategies that may better support student learning
- Ensure accountability and continuous improvement through regular IEP reviews.

Legal and ethical considerations

IEPs are protected by law, ensuring that students with disabilities receive equitable access to education. Schools have a legal and ethical obligation to uphold these plans, creating an inclusive learning environment that supports all students. Parents and caregivers have the right to be active participants in the development, review and modification of their child's IEP, reinforcing a partnership approach to student success.

By maintaining a well-structured and regularly updated IEP, schools can ensure that students with disabilities receive the individualised support they need to succeed academically, socially and emotionally.

School reports

Brace yourself. School reports are tough reading.

Sometimes it takes me a couple of days to work up to reading our child's reports when they arrive. I also need a couple of days to recalibrate after I have read them. Some years I don't read the reports at all, as I don't believe they matter that much. Progress, not perfection – and not all progress is academic.

When you read your child's report, remember the good times through the year – the progress you have witnessed. Recall the 'phases' that you thought would never end, that did this year.

Some years my child has had great interest and progress in literacy or maths, and some years he stagnates. Some years he has really enjoyed some specialist subjects, and other years we barely get into the classroom.

The learning gap

The learning gap between neurotypical children and those with special needs often widens as children progress through their academic journey. While early intervention and support can help mitigate this disparity, research indicates that the cumulative effect of learning differences becomes more pronounced with each passing year.

When children process information more slowly or differently to their peers, each new concept becomes more challenging as learning is sequential, building upon previous knowledge. The learning gap expands further due to attendance issues for medical appointments, therapy sessions and health-related absences. Additionally, challenges with focus, attention and communication can limit how much instructional time children effectively engage with, even when physically present in class.

The learning gap keeps me up at night. I see that gap growing more and more each day.

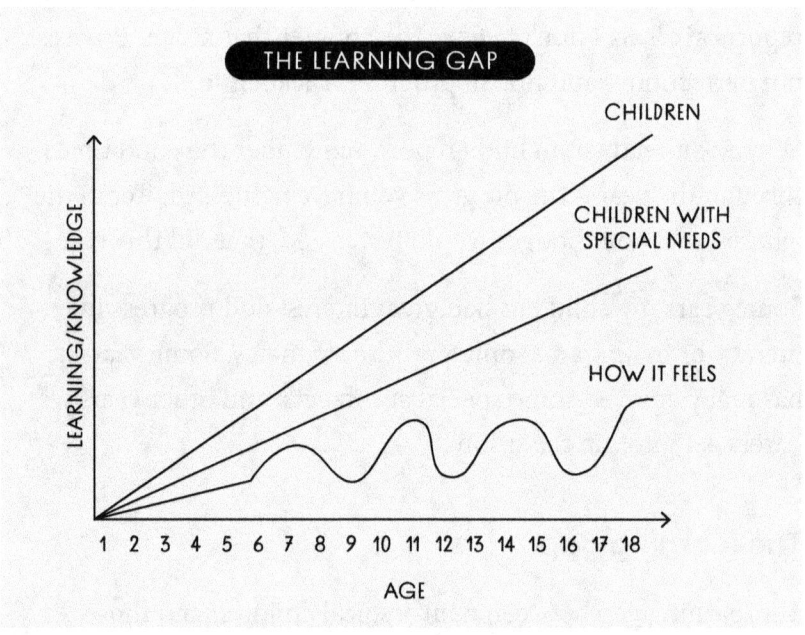

That said, all children learn differently. By the time my child is 18 he will have mastered more than I will be able to fathom. There will be a gap, but I don't think it will matter.

Again, all children learn differently. I say it again, because you do need to remember this and so do I.

Every classroom contains students with widely varying abilities, even among neurotypical children. When your child has special needs, these differences can become even more apparent. The good news is that effective teachers use differentiation to help all students learn successfully. Differentiation simply means tailoring teaching approaches to individual needs rather than expecting every child to learn the same way. When your child's teacher provides different ways to engage with learning materials – whether through visual supports, hands-on activities or technology – they're helping your child process information in ways that match their unique learning style.

Kids learn at different paces. When your child needs extra time to grasp important concepts, differentiation gives them this breathing space before moving on to new material. This prevents small gaps from becoming bigger headaches down the track.

Every child has strengths and challenges. Good differentiation builds on what your child does well while supporting areas where they struggle, building confidence alongside academic skills. You might notice your child receiving modified worksheets, participating in small group activities, or using special technology that helps them access learning in ways that work for them.

If you're worried that your child's learning needs aren't being met, have a chat with their teacher about differentiation strategies they're using or could try out. Sharing your observations about how your child learns best can provide valuable insights to help bridge any learning gaps in the classroom.

Chapter summary

- Setting goals for special-needs children requires flexibility. Traditional goals may need adaptation as timing and measurement can be challenging.

- Individual Education Plans (IEPs) are legally binding documents that outline your child's needs, goals and required adjustments with regular review opportunities.

- School reports can be emotionally difficult. Give yourself time to process them and remember that progress isn't always academic.

- The learning gap between neurotypical and special-needs children often widens over time due to the cumulative effect of processing differences.

- Classroom differentiation helps overcome learning gaps by tailoring teaching approaches to individual needs through multiple engagement strategies and flexible pacing.

CHAPTER 5
CREATING A TEAM

The saying 'it takes a village to raise a child' takes on a whole new meaning when your child has additional needs. For us, that village has evolved into a coordinated team of professionals, educators and family members all working towards common goals.

When our child started primary school, I quickly realised that success wouldn't come from any single person's efforts – not mine, not his teacher's, not the classroom aides', not his therapists'. Instead, it would emerge from the collective expertise, understanding and commitment of everyone involved in his education and development.

Building this team hasn't always been straightforward. It has required ongoing communication, mutual respect and a shared vision. There have been personnel changes, differing opinions and occasional miscommunications. But when everyone has pulled together – when the classroom teacher understands the speech pathologist's strategies, when the school leadership supports the teacher's recommendations, when home and school environments reinforce the same skills – that's when we've seen the most significant progress.

Throughout our journey, I've learned that creating an effective team isn't just about assembling the right professionals. It's about fostering genuine relationships where everyone feels valued and heard. It's about establishing clear channels of communication and ensuring everyone understands their role in supporting your child. Most importantly, it's about maintaining a united front where your child's wellbeing and development remain at the centre of every decision.

This chapter explores how to build and nurture the team that will support your child's mainstream schooling journey – from working with classroom teachers to making the most of Student Support Group (SSG) meetings and navigating the sometimes challenging conversations that arise along the way.

The classroom teacher

The classroom teacher is the most important person in your special-needs child's life after you, their parents.

I want my child to have a teacher who is keen to work with them.

I want my child to have a teacher who understands what a child like mine can contribute to a classroom.

I want my child to have a teacher who is interested in our journey.

Your child needs to trust their teacher explicitly, connect with them deeply, and be seen by them. This is no small feat. However, teachers are superheroes, and this is what they do.

The right teacher will change your special-needs child. The right teacher will help them progress and develop. The right teacher will use the school supports to support your child.

If you fall in love with your child's teacher, it will help your child, too. Speak well about the teacher. Speak highly of the school. Value learning. Be excited with and for them.

Treat the teacher like you are partners in this together. They will spend a lot of time with your child so will get to know them well, and will especially get to know how they learn. Share with them the honest truth about your child and what is going on at home – even if it's just a bad night's sleep or an out-of-routine event the night before – as this affects them when they get to school.

The classroom teacher is also your key to classroom support for your child. A good teacher can:

- Ensure that the support works to your child's advantage
- Ensure the support staff understand how your child learns
- Advocate for your child within the school
- Team your child up with other students who can support them
- Prepare your child and other students for out-of-the-ordinary factors coming up such as excursions, events and changes to the schedule.

Research suggests the longer you can stay with a teacher the better it will be for your child. This is known as looping. Looping can have many benefits for students including improved academic performance, reduced absenteeism, improved behaviour, increased job satisfaction for teachers and teachers becoming student specialists. This is very easy to arrange in schools that have composite classes. We have advocated for our child to stay with the same teacher for a second year where possible and I highly recommend it. They can't promise it, but I raise it as an ideal situation.

No matter what, learn to work *with* the teacher, not against them. They are the key to your child's success. The better they know you and your child the better they can support and advocate for your family.

TEACHER INSIGHT

As a teacher with over 13 years of experience in mainstream education I consider the most important aspect to educational success to be relationship-building: developing my relationship with the child, the parents/guardians/caregivers and with any allied health workers involved in supporting the child's educational journey. Every classroom has a diverse range of needs requiring flexibility, modification and adjustments to support students in accessing the learning. Many of the adjustments and modifications used to support students with special needs also support those without. Visual timetables, routines, social stories and multimodal communication tools have all enhanced my students' learning across the board.

My experience teaching children with additional needs has varied over the years. I have found that open communication with families, previous teachers and allied health professionals, extensive background knowledge about who the child is, and many opportunities to meet with the child prior to the year commencing have been essential in catering to the child's needs. There are important conversations that need to occur, meetings, challenging moments when setting goals and difficulties in ensuring the child's social, emotional and academic needs are being met. These are all outweighed by the joys of building connection, observing new learning taking place, overcoming barriers and discovery. This is where consistent communication among the team is fundamental. The support and involvement of the family positively impacts not only our role as educators but the outcomes that can be achieved by the students.

I have witnessed many success stories in mainstream schooling students with special needs. Despite the extra work involved in supporting their education, celebrating students' achievements and knowing they are set up for success as they continue their educational journey is the greatest joy as a teacher.

Luca Dickinson
Classroom teacher

Student Support Groups

Student Support Groups (SSGs) are formal, regular meetings that bring together all the key people involved in supporting a child with additional needs in a school setting. They typically include parents/caregivers, classroom teachers, school leadership, sometimes the education support staff and, when possible, the relevant specialists (such as speech pathologists, psychologists and OTs). SSGs aim to collaboratively review progress, set goals, update IEPs, and address any concerns or challenges that have arisen since the previous meeting.

SSGs are so important. Don't let a term go by without one.

The biggest challenge is always finding a good time for everyone, but it's worth the effort to get everyone in the room (whether in person or virtual) at the same time. When everyone is together on a regular basis working as a team, that's when the real magic happens.

Our family's SSGs are hybrid, with the allied health professionals on Zoom/Teams and me and the school staff in the school office. I always try to attend in person (and take snacks to share). So much off-the-record conversation happens before and after the official meeting, and I want to get everything I can out of it.

A good way to run an SSG is for everyone who works with your child to give an update. Most SSGs also address progress towards the IEP and any other issues.

Be prepared for a surprise in every meeting. You may hear about something you didn't know had happened, or find the school wants to discuss an issue you might not have been aware of. Be prepared to come out of the meeting feeling slightly dazed.

Most schools will follow up the SSG with notes and a revised IEP. I also like a meeting with actionable items for attendees. If I have any action points from the meeting, I try to tick them off within a week to ensure they are not forgotten. I've also found the quicker I come back with my completed action points, the more likely the other attendees will attend to theirs.

Parent/teacher meetings

A parent/teacher meeting is a great opportunity to be one-on-one with your child's teacher; to get to know more about them, and give them more information about your child and your family. I have found the more I can impart on the teacher about our child, his interests and his strengths, the more the teacher will be able to support, engage with and educate my child. I want them to get a good sense of me and my parenting, too, so they connect with us and our family. Each school teacher we have becomes part of our journey.

Unlike when I went to school, parent/teacher meetings now include the child. This means your child has a voice in their education. Even if they are not verbal, it is probably good for them to attend like the other students, as they can listen and understand what is being said about them.

Again, expect a surprise or two at these meetings. You will find out something you didn't know, or something you should be doing that you weren't aware of. That is okay – you can't be on top of everything that goes on every day at school. Much like with SSGs, I find there is a flurry of things I need to do for our child based on the new information I have learned in the parent/teacher meeting.

Ensure you remind the teacher of your key goals for your child and family in these meetings. As I shared in chapter 4, one of our goals has been to develop our child's reading. I ensure I check that reading is happening every day at school and is a priority. The more I ask about it the more it reminds the teacher how important it is. Let's not forget they are probably being reminded about things for up to 30 other children, so don't feel like you are asking for too much!

Other meetings

Let's be honest: it is never good news when the school asks for you to come in for a meeting at other times. And they will. They will have to tell you about changes to teachers, changes to funding, behaviour concerns and more. They will try to do this face-to-face as everyone knows that this is more effective. Hold on to your hat, as no year will pass without something coming up!

No matter what the bad news is, give yourself three days to calm down and process the news or information. See if you can hold off on responding or reacting for that time. Most issues are manageable after some thinking time, and may not seem like the end of the world as you initially thought. Before you become a keyboard warrior or go nuclear, ask yourself how much this will matter to you and your child in five years.

If there are things you want to discuss with the school, ask to meet at a designated time rather than trying to have a rushed conversation before or after school. Tell them in advance what you'd like to discuss. Some teachers will have minimal experience with parents *and* minimal experience with children with additional needs or parents of children with additional needs. In many cases these teachers will need support in the meeting from a senior teacher, or the assistant principal or principal. (How to make a chat a little more formal and stressful for everyone!) That being said, if there is an issue, raise it. Be the 'difficult parent'.

TEACHER INSIGHT

I have taught in mainstream primary schools for nearly 20 years. Every class I have taught has had at least one or two children with additional needs. In my first class, I had a student who had multiple diagnoses. When I met with his kinder teacher before school started, I began to wonder if I was going to cope.

I felt overwhelmed on my first day with the class as not only did I have parents peering through the windows to check out the new graduate teacher, but I had an aide, a behaviour support specialist and OT in my classroom. I guess as a novice teacher I wanted to learn solo, to let my mistakes go by unnoticed and not feel others were looking at me. I was not in the right mindset as I was holding onto an ideal of a 'perfect classroom' and me, the 'perfect teacher'.

Fortunately, the student and his carer helped me change my thinking. I learned that aiming for perfection was futile. This did not mean giving up on expectations but rather looking for what could work. It meant working with parents and carers to establish what could be improved on, what could be considered progress and what was worth letting go, even if it had worked the previous month. I would not have learned this vital lesson so quickly without the help of a student with additional needs.

I also learned that the parents and carers who alert you to their child's needs early are the ones who put you in the best position to cater for that student. Other teachers and school leadership teams sometimes disagree with this, arguing that every year is new and we shouldn't judge a child based on what has occurred in the past. I disagree;

forewarned is forearmed. The sooner you can begin making connections and finding out what is important to a student and their family, the sooner you can start helping that student progress, learn and be part of their classroom and school community.

Caroline Heath
Literacy specialist

Chapter summary

- The classroom teacher is your biggest ally. Do what you can to support them so they can support and advocate for your child.

- SSGs each term are crucial. Get everyone in the room, take good notes and follow up quickly on any action items that come out of them.

- Parent/teacher meetings are valuable opportunities to connect one-on-one with your child's teacher – make the most of them.

- When challenging situations arise, give yourself three days rule to process the information before responding – most issues become more manageable with time and perspective.

- Remember that most teachers are willing to learn and adapt to support your child – provide them with specific, actionable information rather than general concerns.

CHAPTER 6
THE 'PROFESSIONALS'

The journey of mainstreaming a child with additional needs inevitably involves a cast of professionals who become regular fixtures in your life – speech pathologists, OTs, psychologists, paediatricians and many others. These specialists bring valuable expertise, but navigating their world comes with its own set of challenges.

From the day we were told we needed to see a paediatrician about our child, I realised our family life would now include a revolving series of appointments, assessments and therapy sessions. These professionals would use terms such as 'deficits' and 'delays' while measuring our child against standardised milestones and benchmarks. It has been confronting and exhausting, yet these same professionals have also provided crucial support and strategies that have helped our child thrive.

What I have learned over the years is that these relationships require careful management. You need to be both grateful for their expertise and assertive about your child's needs. You need to coordinate their sometimes conflicting advice and integrate their strategies into everyday life. And, perhaps most importantly, you need to remember that while these professionals see your child through the lens of their specialty, you see your whole child – their personality, their interests, their unique way of being in the world.

This chapter explores how to navigate relationships with the various professionals who support your child's mainstream education journey. We'll look at managing the deficit model that dominates disability services, coordinating therapy within the school day, maintaining productive relationships with therapists, and handling the inevitable transitions when therapists move on.

The deficit model

If your family is like ours, you'll have been in and out of doctors', paediatricians' and specialists' offices from the moment someone told you they thought your child may be experiencing some issues.

Our child has done hundreds of hours of therapy. He spends more time learning than other kids his age. He is watched and corrected more than other children, too.

We spend our days trying to make our children 'better': to fit in or talk like the rest of us. We spend our time talking about what our children *can't* do instead of talking about what they *can* do.

Our children are measured and funded based on their deficits, not their strengths.

The deficit model asks us to see our kids through the lens of what's 'missing' or what needs to be 'fixed'. In our relentless pursuit of therapies, corrections and interventions, we risk overlooking the whole child – their unique perspectives, inherent strengths and natural ways of being in the world.

When we fund based on deficits rather than celebrating capabilities, we perpetuate a system that measures human worth by proximity to an arbitrary 'normal'. Perhaps the greatest shift we can make is not in our children, but in ourselves – moving from a mindset of constant correction to one of radical acceptance, where difference isn't a deficit but simply another way of experiencing the world.

Our kids don't need to be fixed; they need to be seen, valued and supported exactly as they are.

The National Disability Insurance Scheme

I am grateful for the National Disability Insurance Scheme (NDIS) every day. It funds a huge number of things for our child that we as a family would not be able to afford otherwise. We are so grateful for the therapists that it has bought into our lives who have supported our child and us on our journey.

Unfortunately, though, the reality is that managing the paperwork and appointments associated with NDIS is a job in itself. The reviews, the receipts, the portal, the renewing of agreements each year – it all takes more organisation than you'd think.

But this book isn't about the NDIS – maybe the next one – so this is all I will say on the topic here.

Coordinating and managing all the people

There is a high chance you and your child have seen and used a fair few health professionals over the years. One of the key changes we encountered when our child started school was that the professionals visited the school to provide therapy, instead of visiting us at home or us travelling to their office. This sounds great in theory; but it's actually very tricky to arrange suitable times for therapists to see your child during the school day. For starters, we needed to avoid recess and lunch, avoid reading time and avoid afternoons later in the week. There are not many feasible options for times after that!

Managing the therapists coming into school is your responsibility – and it isn't easy. I always wanted our child to see our speech pathologist instead of going to Italian class, but that was near impossible to arrange so I gave up early on that one. Also keep in mind the year goes by so quickly. You are lucky to get in 40 sessions per year (ten weeks per term). The first two weeks of the year are write-offs. Then there are public holidays and sickness to contend with.

I like to arrange any new therapists to visit us at home during the school holidays to see our set-up. However, this is more of a chat with me rather than a session with our child. We don't do formal school holiday sessions because our child finds it confusing to see the therapist out of context. Therapy at school is now his context!

School staff such as your child's teacher are not in the sessions with the therapist, so it can be hard to know what they are doing and how they are progressing. I rely on the reports I receive after the school sessions. I read every one, and like to ensure they lead with an overarching comment on how the session went overall. You do also need to be checking in with the therapists to ensure everyone is on the same page. If the therapist can come to the SSGs this is a good start, and helps to ensure everyone is working towards the same goals.

The more your therapists are aware of what is going on at school, the more they can help and get involved, too. Ensure they are looped into emails about issues that are occurring or upcoming events that your child may need to be supported through. Our speech therapist and OT have access to our child's Compass Education school record which helps to keep them in the loop. Ensure you are empowering your therapists to advocate for your child, too. We recently asked our OT to be more heavily involved in our child's year-level transition. She had some extra time available to help, and worked the transition into her sessions. She also helped the classroom teacher construct the social story. It helped a lot having a new yet experienced team member working on the transition with us and our child.

Most of all, expect the best from your therapists. Challenge them to do their best work with your child. Ask them for progress against goals. Ask them for their views and opinions. Ask them to suggest strategies when times are tough. The more you involve them, the more they can do to help.

THERAPIST INSIGHT

Even with nearly 15 years of experience, there is a constant need to learn, refine my skills and stay up-to-date with the latest evidence-based practices. Being an

OT – or any allied health professional, for that matter – is an ongoing learning journey, guided by the collaborative support of a child by their dedicated team.

In a school-based setting, I am fortunate to work closely with parents, teachers, support staff and specialists, respecting the wealth of knowledge each individual brings. Achieving success would not be possible without the support of every single team member. Each person contributes a unique perspective and skill set, and when working together in harmony, extraordinary progress is made. School visits allow therapists to support skill development in real-life contexts, which facilitates smoother transfer of those skills. However, the success of these visits is reliant on frequent communication, ensuring everyone stays informed about a child's evolving needs and progress, with ongoing adjustments to the therapy plan.

Every child, regardless of their needs, is capable of success. Our role is simply to guide them on their journey to reach it. Being part of a child and their family's journey as they reach their goals, no matter how small they may be, is truly priceless.

Samantha Adler
Paediatric occupational therapist
Inspire 2 Learn

Changing therapists

Sometimes in life, we have to change therapists. There are many reasons why this might happen:

- **Growing up:** Yes, our children grow up. The therapist who looked after us when our child was first diagnosed as a three-year-old might not be the right therapist when the child is nine or ten and is experiencing different issues. I am expecting that once our child gets closer to adolescence I will be looking for therapists who specialise in this age group. There is a big difference in how you work with a toddler and a teenager.
- **Inertia:** This can be on the therapist or the child's part. Too much familiarity or time together can lead to inertia, where neither is pushing the other.
- **They are leaving you:** It's true: therapists will sometimes 'break up' with you and your child. Sometimes they move away. Sometimes they can't service the school. Sometimes they change employers. Sometimes they go on parental leave. It hurts; I have cried every time a therapist has left us. But it does happen and usually isn't personal.
- **Not the right fit anymore:** Yes, I am being polite. Sometimes therapists take the piss, or you sense your child is not as important to them as other children or work issues they're experiencing. When this happens, it is time to either speak with their manager or vote with your feet: leave and find someone else to support your child.

Shit happens, and it can be rough. Give yourself a couple of days and then find yourself a new therapist. No matter what, explain the change to your child in a way they will understand and, if possible, get pictures of the new therapist to start creating a new social story as soon as you can.

If you're unsure where to start in finding a new therapist, ask the school. There are plenty of other therapists coming in and out of the school daily. They will have a few they trust and know do a good job. Also, the more students they are coming to the school for, the less the NDIS travel fee will be, which is better for everyone!

Chapter summary

- The medical world runs on deficits, but our children are so much more than what they can't do. Remember to celebrate their strengths.

- The NDIS is a blessing but managing it is a job in itself. Stay organised with the paperwork.

- School therapy sessions are tricky to coordinate and manage but worth doing. Keep pushing for them to happen.

- Expect the best from your therapists and keep them in the loop. Get them involved in SSGs and school-related planning where possible.

- Sometimes you need to change therapists and that's okay. Whether they're moving on or it's not working anymore, be ready to find someone new.

CHAPTER 7

MANAGING ALL THE THINGS

If parenting is like juggling, then parenting a child with additional needs in mainstream schooling is like juggling while riding a unicycle on a tightrope. The sheer volume of administrative tasks, communications, appointments, school events and daily routines can be overwhelming even for the most organised among us.

When my child started school, I naively thought the paperwork and coordination would decrease. Instead, I found myself managing a growing network of professionals, navigating school systems, tracking medications, planning for special events and constantly preparing for the next transition. Some days it felt like a full-time job on top of my actual job – not to mention the everyday responsibilities of parenting, working and running a household.

What I have learned through this journey is that while you can't eliminate the complexity, you can develop systems to manage it. You can prioritise what truly matters for your child's wellbeing and education while letting some things go. You can anticipate predictable challenges and prepare for them, reducing the stress of last-minute scrambles. And, perhaps most importantly, you can recognise your own limits and set boundaries that protect your family's quality of life.

This is not about achieving perfect organisation or never dropping a ball – it's about finding sustainable ways to manage the increased load that comes with supporting a child with additional needs through mainstream schooling. It's about making strategic choices that maximise your child's opportunities while preserving your own wellbeing.

This chapter explores practical strategies for managing the many moving parts of your child's school experience – from handling the daily flood of communications to navigating special events, transitions, NAPLAN, medication management and more. While the logistics may feel overwhelming at times, with the right approaches, they can become manageable parts of your family's school journey.

Meetings, admin and emails

I wish I had a magic wand or another day in my week to help me manage all the things, but I don't.

Managing our child and his disability is a full-time job some days. Between the school requirements, the NDIS and attending to his personal needs there is not much time for other things, especially me.

Like everyone, I receive a lot of emails, phone calls and text messages. In a normal day there are a lot of requests of me, things to do and things to remember. I have some rules of thumb to help manage this:

- If an email or text only requires a short reply, I do it straight away.
- If an email or text requires me to do something that I can't attend to in the moment, or requires multiple steps, I write it on a list so I remember it. I also try to do the first part of a multi-step task as soon as I receive the message – for example, if I learn that school swimming is going to clash with a speech therapy session, I will email the speech therapist's diary coordinator to find another time for that week.
- If the email or text is an FYI, I do try to read it then and there and, if possible, respond with a comment to acknowledge it.

I try to schedule school meetings after drop-off or before pick-up if possible, to save myself from having to travel back and forth to school multiple times. I find the days when I need to go to school more than twice are very tiring. The less I overload myself, the better everyone in our family will function.

Be present

Yep, I know: eye roll. But it does work.

Being present is more than putting down your mobile phone. It's about turning up.

Be seen. Show to the school and teachers you are invested in your child, the school and the outcomes. Read the newsletters; read *all* the emails. Ensure that your child has an orange T-shirt for Harmony Day. Turn up to the curriculum sessions. Be on the journey with your child.

The more you are present, the more it sends a message to your child about the importance of school, and the more it sends the school a message that you are engaged and willing to do what's needed to ensure your child is supported.

Medication

Many children with special needs require medication to help manage their conditions, whether for ADHD, epilepsy, anxiety or other health concerns. Medication can play a crucial role in supporting your child's ability to function, learn and participate at school, though the decision to medicate is often complex and personal.

Schools need to know about any medications your child takes, even if administered at home, as it helps them understand your child's needs and any potential side effects or issues that might arise during school hours. You will be asked to provide medical information in writing, usually through the school's medical information forms at enrolment or when medication changes.

For medication that needs to be given during school hours (including on excursions or school camps):

- Schools require a written medication authority form that includes details from your doctor about the medication, dosage and timing.

- Medication must be provided in the original pharmacy-labelled container.
- The school needs clear information about any specific storage requirements (such as refrigeration).
- Staff who administer medication need to be trained and will keep records of each dose given.
- Schools usually store medication in a secure location.

Most schools have specific policies about:

- Which staff members can administer medication
- Where and how medication is stored
- Emergency procedures if there are any medication-related issues
- Documentation requirements for each dose given
- Procedures for excursions and school camps.

It is important to keep the school updated about any changes to your child's medication routines. Also, discuss with them a plan for any potential missed doses or what to do if your child needs medication unexpectedly during school hours. You will need to plan ahead with the school for camps and other off-site school situations.

PARENT INSIGHT

'Is it a game-changer?' she asked.

My heart sank. I was talking to a friend, two weeks into starting ADHD medication for my six-year-old. The truth was, so far, this process had yielded only anxiety, guilt and a lot of judgement (both external and self-inflicted).

From a young age Ted had boundless energy, bouncing around our house knocking things over in his need to move his body. My husband and I joked that he was like a dog: we had to run him! There were other clues, too: his 'tantrums' were off the charts compared to other kids; he hyperfocused on areas of interest and yet had no ability to focus when he wasn't interested. But he was our funny, kind little encyclopedia (via him I know more about dinosaurs than any person in the known universe) and he'd give almost anyone a go.

We loved him fiercely and felt protective. Looking back, it's clear that his daycare and kinder teachers raised questions, but we batted them away – why would anyone question the development of a preschooler with the vocab of a professor!

Within the Covid madness we were lucky to have an unfailingly kind prep teacher who gently noted his need to move a lot, his trouble focusing and his 'big feelings' in interactions with peers. Finally she asked if I'd ever considered seeing an OT. I'd grown weary of people talking in hushed tones and asking me vague questions about my child, so I asked her to give it to me straight.

'Ted can't sit on the mat for even one minute,' she told me.

'Oh … and is that unusual for a six-year-old boy?'

'Yes.'

So began the process of diagnosis: OT, GP, paediatrician. This book covers these topics, and I concur 100 per cent that you have to do your research and be your child's advocate. At the end of months of waiting (waiting lists are impossible!) it was confirmed: Ted has ADHD.

So what did we do? We had lots of options: OT, psychologist, diet, supplements, sensory supports and so on. We tried them all and some of them helped a bit. I was desperate to avoid medication, even though statistically it has the greatest chance of 'success'. But things were getting dire at school: the hyperactivity and emotional dysregulation were making it difficult for the class to function. Finally a friend asked me if I would be so reluctant to try medication if Ted had diabetes. Good point, I thought! So we decided to try, safe in the knowledge that if it didn't work, we could stop.

I'd assumed medicating our child would require us to follow a clear scientific process, and the doctor would know the right drug and how much to give. Nope. It was a long process, starting on one drug, slowly creeping it up, monitoring any changes and talking to the school constantly, then changing and starting again. There were definitely improvements along the way, but it took us two years to get it right and it needs monitoring and tweaking as he grows. I genuinely think that without medication our school journey would have been impossible, but it isn't a cure-all. We still have hard days and combine medication with many non-medical options.

So, yes, for us it has been a game-changer, but it's been a long and continuous journey to change this game.

Genevieve
Mother of two boys

School events

OMG. There are so many school events.

Be prepared for:

- Multiple sports days: athletics, swimming, cross country
- School theatre productions/musicals
- Camps/overnights
- Dress-up days and school parades – Harmony Day, Halloween and more
- Excursions
- Swimming lessons/surfing lessons
- And more!

Does your child need to attend everything? No. These activities are all optional. My advice is to choose what you feel your child can do (and wants to do) and say no to the rest.

In foundation year we did everything, but it burned out my child and me. We have learned to pick and choose what is best for him depending on the time of the year.

Remember that every one of these activities is out of routine and will need to be planned for.

School excursions and camps deserve special consideration. Every child has the right to attend these activities, and schools have an obligation to make reasonable adjustments for inclusion.

Excursions tend to be shorter outings but still require preparation. Talk through with your child what will happen on the day, who will be supervising and any activities planned.

For children who struggle with transitions or new environments, a visual schedule about the excursion can be extremely helpful.

Camps offer valuable experiences for children to build independence and social skills, though they may present unique challenges and need even more planning. Reasonable adjustments might include having your child only do the day part, the school assigning a dedicated support person, creating a visual timetable of activities, allowing quiet time breaks or modifying physical activities to ensure participation. Some families find it helpful to visit the campsite beforehand or provide familiar items from home to ease anxiety.

Remember that these experiences are meant to be enjoyable learning opportunities. If modifications are needed to make them accessible for your child, don't hesitate to advocate for these adjustments.

Transitions

We discussed the kinder-to-school transition in chapter 3, but I think it's important to discuss transitions for special-needs children more generally.

I find change hard, and I am an adult. I can't imagine how difficult it is for my special-needs child.

Research shows that difficulty with transitions often stems from:

- Challenges with executive functioning
- Anxiety about new situations
- Difficulty processing sensory changes in the environment
- Problems with time management and sequencing
- Attachment to routines and predictability.

Some strategies to consider include:

- **Visual supports:** An individualised visual schedule helps children understand and predict the sequence of activities in their day. Visual times can make abstract time concepts more concrete, helping children understand how long they have until a change occurs. Social stories (our favourite), either through pictures or a narrative, help explain new situations and expected behaviours.

- **Structured preparation:** Children benefit from receiving advance notice of changes through multiple cues, including verbal and visual. Practice runs of new routines help build familiarity and confidence. Gradually exposing children to new environments or experiences allows them to adjust at their own pace. Clear markers for the beginning and end of activities help with understanding sequence, while consistent transition signals or songs can be helpful cues for change. Creating predictable routines helps children feel secure during changes.

- **Environmental strategies:** Reducing sensory input during transition times can prevent overwhelm, while having a designated quiet space available allows children to safely retreat when needed. Maintaining some familiar elements in new situations helps create bridges between different environments. Transition objects, such as comfort items, can also provide emotional support during change.

- **Communication:** Using clear, concrete language helps children understand what is happening and what is expected. Breaking down transition steps into manageable chunks makes them less overwhelming. Positive reinforcement during transitions helps build confidence and motivation.

Regular check-ins during periods of change allow parents and teachers to monitor how the child is coping and adjust support as needed. Consistent communication between home and school ensures everyone is working together effectively.

Successful transition depends on thorough individual assessment of the child's specific needs, and strong collaboration between family, school and support services. Consistent implementation of chosen strategies, regular monitoring of progress and a gradual approach to building the child's skills and confidence make all the difference.

Transitioning from Year 2 to Year 3

Academic expectations increase notably in Year 3. Students move from early learning approaches to more independent work and complex thinking. There is a greater emphasis on reading to learn rather than learning to read. Writing tasks become more detailed and structured, and mathematical concepts become more abstract. This is also the first year students participate in NAPLAN testing (which we'll discuss in the next section).

The teaching style changes in Year 3, too. There is typically less play-based learning and hands-on activities, with more emphasis on formal instruction and independent work. Students are expected to manage their time better, follow multi-step instructions and take more responsibility for their learning. Class discussions become more complex, and students are expected to contribute more sophisticated ideas.

Social and emotional development is also significant at this age. Students are expected to show more maturity in their behaviour and relationships. They need to develop better self-regulation skills and work more independently. There will also be more events that students will have the opportunity to participate in (or not), including district sports and school camps. This can be particularly challenging for students with disabilities or developmental differences who might need more support with all of these things.

For students with disabilities, the transition to Year 3 will require additional planning and support to ensure they can adapt to the increased expectations.

NAPLAN

The National Assessment Program – Literacy and Numeracy (NAPLAN) is the standardised testing program that assesses all Australian students in Years 3, 5, 7 and 9. NAPLAN tests reading, writing, language conventions (spelling, grammar and punctuation) and numeracy. It provides a point-in-time snapshot of how students are performing against national standards.

You will hear a lot about NAPLAN and it's worth considering your family's stance on it. My opinion is that it is just one test on one day. It doesn't measure creativity, critical thinking or many other important skills. It also doesn't affect school grades or progression. It is used by schools to show their academic ability and by the government for general trends and funding purposes.

Parents can withdraw their child from NAPLAN if they have a diagnosed disability. This decision should be made in consultation with the school. Formal exemption paperwork will need to be completed by both parties.

We have chosen for our child not to complete NAPLAN. We didn't want to impose another new process he would have to learn to complete the tests. We also believe our child does not need the extra stress to complete something that tests him. We don't need to know how he is progressing against the national standards.

Students with disabilities or learning difficulties can participate in NAPLAN with adjustments. These adjustments might include:

- Extra time
- Rest breaks
- Use of a scribe
- Use of assistive technology
- Alternative-format test papers (such as braille or large print)
- Small group or individual supervision
- Access to a support person.

The key is that any adjustments should reflect the support normally provided for classroom assessments. You should discuss options with the school before the NAPLAN testing period.

After-school care

Every child has the right to access Outside School Hours Care (OSHC), and services must make reasonable adjustments to support children with disabilities so they can participate.

The funding landscape includes several options to support inclusion. Services can apply for support funding to provide the additional staff or resources necessary to support your child. Families may be also able to utilise their NDIS funding to support this, while the Child Care Subsidy can also help with general costs.

In our family we have arranged our work days so that we don't need to send our child to after-school care. We find he can only cope with the school day and needs to come home as soon as possible to self-regulate from his day at school.

Setting up care requires careful planning and communication. Even though care is usually offered on site at school, OSHC is not the school's responsibility and it's another party you will need to manage! You should arrange a meeting with the service coordinator to discuss your child's specific needs and support requirements. This meeting should cover sharing relevant medical plans, support plans and behaviour management strategies that work. It's also important to discuss any personal care requirements and establish clear emergency procedures.

After-school services have specific responsibilities they must fulfill. This includes ensuring staff are appropriately trained to support children with additional needs and that any required medical or personal care support is consistently available. If you find that a service isn't meeting your child's needs or is refusing to make reasonable adjustments, you have a right to advocacy and should raise this as an issue. After-school care is a service that students with disabilities should be able to access.

Surviving school holidays

Children with special needs, particularly those who are autistic or have other neurodevelopmental conditions, often find comfort and security in the predictable routines of school. The transition to school holidays can be challenging as it disrupts these established patterns. Children might experience anxiety, behavioural changes or emotional dysregulation. The sudden shift from structured days to unstructured time can be particularly challenging for students who rely on routines to feel secure and regulated.

Some strategies to help manage school holidays include:

- **Creating a visual holiday schedule:** These do help. Include any planned activities.
- **Maintain some elements of routine:** This might be keeping to similar meal and snack times or maintaining familiar bedtime routines.
- **Planning the transition:** Gradually adjust your routines in the run-up to school holidays.
- **Maintaining social connections:** This is very important to do if you can, through planned activities.

Balance all of this with a heap of R&R, which means iPad time for our child!

Returning to school, especially after summer holidays, also requires support and preparation.

Chapter summary

- Managing school and disability needs is intense. Handle emails quickly, plan meetings smartly and keep good systems in place.

- Choose school events wisely. Not everything needs to be attended, so pick what works for your child and family.

- Year 3 brings big changes with more academic pressure. Plan ahead and know it's okay to skip NAPLAN if it's not right for your child.

- After-school care needs careful planning. Work with providers to help them meet your child's needs, but remember home time might be what your child needs most.

- School holidays can be tricky. Keep some routines going but balance structure with plenty of downtime and iPad breaks.

CHAPTER 8
FINDING A TRIBE

Before we explore how to help our children find their social place, let's hear directly from a student with autism about how he experiences the world:

> ### STUDENT INSIGHT
> Being neurodiverse means your brain works more different than the average human. It's like having more powers than the average human. A thing to be appreciated instead of discomfited for.
>
> My autism boosts my senses. I have a very strong sense of smell which means I can smell things others can't. But there can also be a downside. Some foods at breakfast smell really bad to me. Sometimes certain socks make me feel uncomfortable, and I don't like the feeling of velvet. It makes me feel all wrong.

> We autistic people have huge emotions. You might feel something heavier. If a mate calls you names and says, 'It's just a joke', for the average person, they'd be like, 'Oh', and continue with their work. For you, you might feel really sad.
>
> When I'm feeling excited, I move my body in different ways. I jump, wave my arms, and do exercises. It helps me keep the excitement in, you know? It makes me feel great.
>
> Sometimes people get too close and pop your personal space bubble. Since we're autistic, it actually overwhelms you a lot, which is very uncomfortable.
>
> We're all different. And that's okay.
>
> *Max*
> *Year 4 student*

One of the most beautiful yet challenging aspects of mainstreaming a child with additional needs is watching them navigate the social landscape of school. While academics and therapies often dominate discussions about special needs education, the importance of friendship and belonging cannot be overstated. Every child deserves to feel connected, valued and part of a community.

For my child, finding his place socially has been a journey with its own timeline. It hasn't always unfolded in the ways I initially imagined or hoped for. I have watched him standing alone in the playground, seen birthday party invitations dwindle as other children formed more complex social groups, and felt that particular ache that comes when you see your child struggling to connect. But I have also witnessed moments of genuine connection, unexpected friendships that bloom across year levels, and the quiet joy that comes when your child finds peers who accept them just as they are.

What I have learned is that social connections for children with additional needs often develop differently – they're not lesser, just different. They may form more slowly, follow unconventional patterns, or look nothing like the friendship groups we remember from our own school days. Finding a tribe isn't just about having lots of friends; it's about having meaningful connections where your child feels safe, understood and appreciated.

This journey isn't just about your child finding their place, either. As parents, we also need our own tribe – other parents who understand the unique challenges and joys of raising a child with additional needs, who don't require explanations or apologies, who can offer both practical support and emotional understanding when the journey gets tough.

This chapter explores strategies for supporting your child's social development at school, navigating the sometimes tricky waters of birthday parties and playdates, and finding your own supportive community along the way.

Taking time

It will take time for your child to develop friendships at school. The reality is that children with special needs process things a lot slower than neurotypical children, therefore many will find a lot of play too quick to follow. Not only that, the play changes too quickly for them to consistently learn the new rules.

Many special-needs children will tend to play by themselves or bounce around from group to group. Most parents of special-needs children I speak to talk about struggles their children have during recess and lunch breaks.

Friendships take time for everyone. They take even longer for special-needs children to make and keep. The more you can support your child in making friendships, the better. It will be easier for your child to develop friendships if they are in the same class with the same children each year, but this isn't always possible in large schools or where there are composite classes. Be proactive in this area. Give the school a list of your child's buddies or friends – not just one name, but several options. Many schools formally request this information before class placements, but if they don't, reach out anyway. Advocate for your child by explaining why certain friendships are important for their sense of security and adjustment. Most schools will try to accommodate at least one friendship connection, understanding how vital this is for a smooth transition.

Explain to your child about friendship – that they take time to develop, and most are based on shared interests. Be upfront with them that it's normal for friendship dynamics to change or for friends to ebb and flow. Friendship can involve more than one person, too, in the case of friendship groups. Group dynamics is an additional layer of complexity you will need to help your child understand.

There are practical ways in which you can support your child to develop friendships. Organise playdates. Attend events (when they are suitable for your child). Invite other children and their parents over. Go to the local park after school and invite others along.

Some children love supported social groups. These specialised groups help children practise key social communication abilities such as turn-taking, reading social cues and expressing emotions appropriately, while connecting them with peers who understand their experiences and challenges. They're a great chance to learn the rules of friendship and social situations in a supportive environment. My child enjoys spending time at our local We Rock the Spectrum sensory gym – an inclusive play space where he can be himself and play freely with others who accept him. Find an option that might work for your child and try it out.

Birthday parties

It hurts when your child doesn't receive birthday party invitations. It will happen. Prepare yourself now to be disappointed.

Many foundation or prep classes will invite the whole class or even the whole year level. I love it when this happens. It's a great way to get to know everyone and usually starts a bit of a trend for the year. I recommend going to these parties if you can. Some of them will be super awkward as your child may not have done lots of parties, and all-class celebrations are big and busy – but give it a go.

I also suggest you consider hosting an all-year or all-class party for your child if this is a trend in their class or year level. If it's during the warmer months, do it at a park, or a play centre in winter. Get the class list from the teacher or invite everyone via the class WhatsApp group.

All-class parties will happen less often as your child ages through the years. The invites will dwindle, but that is okay. The parties will also change from park events to activities, such as bowling and roller skating, as children get older. We took our child ten-pin bowling one school holidays, knowing that a bowling party was coming up. When the party happened, our child knew what to expect and had a great day with his friends. We also take him back to places that we experienced during parties, such as play centres, for him to have a play in a quieter scenario.

I always stay and watch over my child at parties. I don't feel comfortable leaving him, even though other parents might drop their children and run. I am happy to help supervise or support the organising parent. And who doesn't want an extra set of hands at a kids' party!

Being the snack parent

One way I have helped our son develop relationships is by being the snack mum. Those who know me know I am not the best cook, but I am pretty organised – so being the snack mum is absolutely in my wheelhouse.

I bring snacks to everything, for everyone. On school excursions and at sports carnivals I have enough snacks for as many people as possible. I bring sweet and savoury snacks to after-school playground missions. I drop off boxes of Chupa Chups at the end of each term for my child to give out. I do try to provide some healthy options too. I find the kids don't really mind what I have, and I never come home with anything left over!

Children are always hungry. Most children don't mind coming up and asking for a snack. At that point I ensure I introduce myself as Remy's mum. Most children are very grateful. On excursions everyone wants to be in a group with us.

Diversify your child's friendship options

In his book *Tricky Kids*, clinical psychologist Andrew Fuller suggests children should have diverse friendship groups with connections from a range of different backgrounds. Diversity supports their resilience and also means they are less likely to be led astray in later years. I think diversity in friendships is particularly important for special-needs children – and I particularly encourage our child to make friends with both neurodiverse and neurotypical children.

Andrew Fuller suggests a range of practical strategies for diversifying your child's peer group including travel, youth groups, broadening your connections with your extended family, changing schools and, in some cases, moving away from the area you live in.

We have found hitting the local park after school a very effective way to meet new friends and diversify our child's friendship circle. He has made friends with children from other year levels – which is great because, while he is a little older than others in his year level, he also enjoys playing with younger children who are closer to his level of play. I have also found more parent friends with children in other year levels which has been good for all of us.

We have chosen not to participate in any after-school extra-curricular activities. We are school-holidays regulars at our local We Rock the Spectrum children's gym. We feel this place diversifies our child's friendship group, while allowing him to meet other kids who share similar interests. We deliberately choose activities that we know are in his interest area – such as water play and climbing activities – as this allows him to meet other children who have similar interests.

PARENT INSIGHT

Watching Jack through his early school years has been such a hard journey. Those first two years were heartbreaking – seeing him struggle to make friends, that awful moment at the friendship bench when no one came to play with him, watching older kids being mean to him during sport. Covid made everything worse, and he became even more isolated even though he was smart and doing well with his schoolwork.

I couldn't just sit back and watch. I got involved in everything at Jack's school – volunteering for anything I could, organising his therapy sessions during lunch so he'd have support in the playground. Some days I wondered if I was being too much, but seeing Jack struggle every day kept me going.

Things started to change slowly. His OT and speech therapist really helped. Then in Year 1, he made a friend – another boy who just understood him – and that changed everything. By Year 2, Jack started making friends with kids in different year levels too. Having older and younger friends gave him so many more options at school and really boosted his confidence.

Year 3 was so much better. His dad went on school camp with him – camp was something I never thought would happen. Jack has real friends now, gets invited to birthday parties, and is doing brilliantly at school. The soccer team I started for him is still going strong. Looking back, I've learnt that sometimes being a mum means you just have to keep fighting for your kid and making things happen.

Sarah Mitchell
Mum to two boys

Finding parent friends

It's not only about your child finding their tribe – you also need to find your tribe among the parents. Again, this takes time, but you will find some parent friends. Your children might not be friends, but if you spend time together they may become friends over time.

You will quickly identify fellow special needs parents at school – they're often the ones lingering until the bell rings to ensure their child enters with everyone else. They're typically waiting patiently at the end of the day, too, as the school's daily responsibility concludes. These brief encounters at drop-off and pick-up times can evolve into meaningful connections.

Another way you can make parent friends is by volunteering. Volunteer for the school excursions and sports carnivals. Volunteer to be class representative. Volunteer to do the sausage sizzle at the next Bunnings event. These are all great opportunities to meet other parents but also to do something that makes you feel good. It also teaches your kids about the importance of community and giving back.

You will pick up parent friends during the special-needs journey, too. Once a term I have coffee and a late breakfast with two special-needs parent friends. These catch-ups feel better than therapy to me. Our children met in early learning, and see each other a couple of times a year, but us parents catch up more regularly.

Finding support and connection is invaluable on your parenting journey. Local support networks, both formal and informal, can provide understanding that others simply cannot. Facebook groups specific to your child's diagnosis or needs can be lifelines during challenging times, offering advice, resources and sometimes just a place to vent with people who truly get it. Many areas also have face-to-face support groups that meet monthly, and some disability-specific organisations run workshops and family days where you can connect with others walking similar paths. These connections often become your most valuable resource, offering both practical solutions and emotional support when you need it most.

Chapter summary

- Special-needs children take longer to develop friendships. Be patient and support your child by organising playdates and explaining friendship dynamics.

- Navigate birthday parties strategically. Attend class-wide events where possible, prepare for fewer invitations as children age and consider hosting inclusive parties yourself.

- Being the 'snack parent' can help facilitate social connections by sharing food at excursions and school events.

- Encourage diverse friendships across different year levels and neurotypes. Choose activities based on your child's interests.

- Find your own parent support network.

CHAPTER 9
THE TOUGH TIMES

No matter how well you prepare, how thoughtfully you choose a school or how dedicated the teaching staff may be, there will inevitably be tough times along your mainstreaming journey. These challenges aren't a sign of failure but rather an expected part of blazing a trail that wasn't designed with your child in mind.

What I have learned through these experiences is that resilience doesn't mean avoiding difficulties – it means developing the capacity to face them, learn from them and adapt accordingly. Sometimes this means advocating more strongly for your child's needs, sometimes it means teaching them new coping strategies and sometimes it means reconsidering your approach entirely.

The tough times can be isolating. It's easy to look around at other families and imagine their school journeys are proceeding smoothly while yours feels like an uphill battle.

This chapter explores how to navigate the inevitable difficult periods in your mainstream schooling journey – from addressing behavioural issues and bullying to understanding school refusal and knowing when to consider alternative educational paths. While these topics might be confronting, being prepared for challenges means you'll be better equipped to face them if and when they arise.

Issues

There will be issues: problems and situations you haven't planned for; incidents you can't change.

How you handle issues and setbacks will make a huge difference to the overall experience for you and your child.

When I encounter an issue with the school that will affect my child – such as a change of teacher mid-year, a rule change or a change in aides – I allow myself to seethe for a day or two, and then get on with problem-solving. I find the best way to handle most things is to ask the school and the professionals in your team, and even google some strategies to deal with it. It is unlikely someone else hasn't experienced a similar situation before.

If the issue is with our own child's behaviour, the first step we take is to have a chat with our child about it. I normally do this in the car when we are both looking straight ahead or out the window, so it feels a little less confrontational. This allows us to broach awkward conversations within an environment where he is a captive audience!

Depending on the issue, we, the school or the OT draw up a social story to explain the undesired behaviour and the desired behaviour. This also shows the school that we are trying to resolve the issue.

My rule of thumb:

- **The first time an issue occurs:** It could have been an accident.
- **The second time the same issue occurs:** I consider what I might not be hearing or listening to in this situation, as it wasn't an accident. More serious action taken.
- **The third time the same issue occurs:** This is a clear indicator there is an ongoing issue. We have a good rethink and make drastic changes. Nothing changes if nothing changes.

This doesn't work for every issue, but it is a good place to start when issues arise. And they will.

Behaviour support plans

There is a high chance your family might experience serious issues during the years of schooling. I am sorry in advance. This will suck and be hard work.

Schools develop behaviour support plans (BSPs; sometimes called individual behaviour management plans) when typical classroom strategies aren't enough to support a student's needs. This usually happens when a child's behaviour is significantly impacting their learning, social relationships or safety at school, or if they have had multiple behaviour incidents or suspensions.

The process starts with the school reaching out to you to discuss observations and concerns. They will want to understand your perspective and any insights you have about your child's behaviour, triggers or what strategies work at home. The school team typically includes the classroom teacher, learning support staff and someone from the school leadership team. Sometimes they might suggest involving regional behaviour specialists from your state or territory department of education, or recommend getting input from external specialists such as psychologists or OTs.

Some schools or states integrate behaviour support into the IEP, while others keep each as a separate document. Regular meetings should occur to review how well the plan is working and for adjustments to be made as needed.

Sometimes the behaviour doesn't improve. Yep. At this point the school needs to seek some more expertise. This might include school psychologists and recommendations for external assessments. The school might also discuss intensive support options such as modified timetables or additional support.

The school should try everything they can in consultation with you.

If there are ongoing issues, they will get more support from the department of education too. They might suggest moving your child to a specialist school for a while. It doesn't have to be forever – some students return to mainstream schools after developing better coping strategies and behavioural regulation skills. And some children end up happy at the new school and stay.

Bullying

Schools are much more inclusive places than they were when we attended. However, bullying is still rife and an issue that a lot of children face – not just neurodivergent or special-needs children.

All bullying must be reported to the school. Most schools have processes to deal with it, but they need to know it occurred to be able to sort it out.

I am a fan of the work of bullying expert Evelyn M Field OAM and her bestselling book, *Bully Blocking* (2023). Evelyn teaches that many victims of bullying do not 'fit in', hence why they are singled out by bullies. To counteract this, we as a family do as much as we can to ensure our child fits in. We buy him the drink bottle everyone at school has. We practise soccer with him as all the boys in his year level play it (he has no interest in soccer, or any sport for that matter). We take him to the swimming pool the weekend before the swimming carnival so he knows what to expect. Does this make a difference? Who knows, but we feel it will ensure he is less likely to be a victim.

Evelyn also suggests enabling your child with some smart retorts to say to a bully if a situation arises. Some of my favourites are:

- 'And?'
- 'Wow!'
- 'Whatever.'
- 'Really?'
- 'Fancy that.'
- 'Life's a bitch.'
- 'I must google that.'
- 'Is there an app for that?'

- 'I think it's bad for your reputation to be seen with a nerd like me.'
- 'If you stand too close, you'll catch my germs.'

Evelyn suggests role-playing the situation with your child in advance. I know a few parents who have done this and it worked well, giving their child confidence in these situations.

Even though our child is limited verbally we have tried to instil this idea. He does rough and tumble practise with dad and is well versed at getting out of physical situations. We also try to give him some phrases to use such as 'get off'. Surprisingly, he can use the f-word when he needs to. We model as much as we can.

Ultimately there will be bullying. Get ready for it. Even if it is not said to your child's face there will be comments made, names called and other snide remarks.

Be the bigger person. Teach your child to be the bigger person, too.

School refusal

School refusal is more complex than typical truancy and has become an increasingly significant challenge in recent years, particularly since Covid. The complexity of school refusal often catches families off guard. What starts with occasional reluctance can quickly develop into an entrenched pattern that becomes harder to address the longer it continues.

School refusal is often rooted in anxiety, sensory issues or emotional distress rather than behaviour deviance. For neurodiverse students, school refusal often stems from specific challenges such as sensory overload in busy school environments, difficulty with social interactions, changes in routine or academic pressures that aren't properly accommodated for their learning style. These students also sometimes experience physical symptoms such as headaches and stomach aches due to heightened stress responses.

Common strategies for addressing school refusal include:

- **Creating a gradual return plan:** Start with short periods at school and slowly build up. For children with additional needs this might need to be even more gradual and include specific accommodations for sensory needs or social challenges.
- **Identifying and addressing specific triggers:** Work with the school to understand exactly what is causing your child distress.
- **Seeking professional support:** Work with psychologists and counsellors who understand the specific challenges of neurodiversity and school refusal. They can help develop coping strategies tailored to the child's needs.
- **Asking for school-based adjustments:** These might include having a safe space to retreat to, more sensory breaks, modified timetables, social skills support or having a support person available.

The path back to school isn't linear: there are often setbacks and challenges along the way. It requires patience, understanding and a coordinated approach between family, the school and support services. The impact extends beyond education, affecting family relationships, parental employment and the student's social development and self-esteem.

Other options

Sometimes the mainstream school option is not going to work or does not work any longer. There are a few options to consider in this case.

Homeschooling

Yep, homeschooling is on the rise in Australia.

Homeschooling can offer significant advantages for special-needs children. It gives you the ability to customise the learning environment and pace. You can adjust lightning, noise levels, seating arrangements and the schedule to meet your child's needs. You can also tailor the curriculum to your child's specific learning style and interests. You are not bound to the one-size-fits-all approach of traditional schooling.

However, you need to be ready to devote the time and energy to homeschool, and use the resources and support services out there. There are many homeschool support groups for special-needs families, so investigate what is in your area. You might also want to see if there are homeschooling activities or social groups that you and your child could get involved in.

There is specific documentation and legal requirements to attend to as a homeschooler. Each state has different homeschool laws and additional requirements for special-needs students. Some also require more detailed documentation or educational plans for special-needs homeschooling students. However, if you are self-managed on the NDIS and can get around that portal, I am sure you can do any paperwork that is thrown at you!

PARENT INSIGHT

As a mother, I had grand plans for what my son would achieve in his schooling career: the friends that he would make and the life he would have; the speeches he would give and the groups he would lead. That vision came crashing down when he received his autism diagnosis.

Initially, we made the extremely difficult decision to send my son to a special-needs school. It was not the dream that most parents have for their firstborn. After two years, academically, he'd outgrown his peers. This was a light at the end of the tunnel – or so we thought.

We transferred him to my daughter's mainstream school with a full-time aide. After a term it became glaringly obvious that it was not the right fit. It was too loud and too bright, and there was too much going on. So we were forced to make another difficult decision: to homeschool.

Faced with thoughts of impostor syndrome and doubt that I, a non-teacher, could do better than the schooling system, we decided to give a go. Three years on and I can safely say it was one of the best decisions we could have made. I am not an amazing teacher, yet I have created a space where our son feels safe enough to thrive, to learn and to step into his education fully. For him, homeschooling isn't a 'nice to have', it's a way of life. Homeschooling has shown me that he can truly be who he wants to be without fear of rejection or ridicule from his peers.

Parents, trust in your gut that you have everything inside of you to make this a reality for your autistic child.

Natalie Karras
Specialist parent coach
You Are Seen

Specialist schools

The other option to consider is a specialist school. In Australia, specialist schools (also called special schools) are part of the education system at both government and non-government levels.

Eligibility is typically determined through formal assessment and consultation with the school and education department. Students usually need to meet specific criteria related to their disability or special educational needs.

Government specialist schools are funded through state and territory education departments and are free to attend, though there may be some additional costs for programs or resources. Each state and territory has its own approach. For example, Victoria has a network of specialist schools across the state, while other states might have fewer dedicated specialist schools but more specialist units within mainstream schools.

Many specialist schools in Australia focus on children with specific needs, whether that be due to autism, physical disabilities, intellectual disabilities, behavioural issues or sensory impairments.

The specialist school curriculum follows the Australian Curriculum but is modified to meet students' needs, with a strong focus on life skills and transition-planning for post-school life.

Transport assistance is often available, too. I hear it takes a term or two to get transport arrangements ('the bus') happening, but once in place it's a huge help and something that the children enjoy.

Changing mainstream schools

In some cases, you might need to change schools. You might need to move locations, or your current school may not be working for your child or your family.

Before the move, gather all the key documentation you will need, including:

- Current learning plans/IEPs
- Recent assessments and specialist reports
- Medical documentation
- Examples of accommodations or adjustments that have worked well
- Recent school reports and any BSPs.

Visit the new school. Talk with the principal. Treat this like you are starting again and ask all the questions:

- How do they handle IEPs?
- What's their approach to integration and inclusion?
- How do they communicate with parents?
- What specialist support staff do they have on board, or access to?
- How do they handle transitions for new students with special needs?

In Australia, if your child has funding, you generally don't need to apply for funding again when moving between mainstream schools, as the funding moves with your child. However, you do need to inform both schools about the existing funding arrangements. Check that the new school understands your child's current level of support. I also suggest you ask to meet with the learning support team at the new school to discuss how the funding will be used and what you think your child needs. While funding follows your child, the new school might allocate or use it differently within their support structure. If you are moving between states, it's worth checking with the new school as there can be some state-specific variations in how funding is implemented. There is also a chance that the school will want to do their own assessments, and the funding will need to be reviewed or reapplied for.

It's hard

Schooling a special-needs child is hard. Issues are hard. School is hard. School holidays are hard.

Parenting is hard enough.

Add special needs and it becomes a lot harder.

Chapter summary

- Issues will pop up and that's normal. Give yourself a few days to process the news before reacting, and remember others have likely faced similar challenges.

- When behaviour becomes a bigger worry, work with the school on support plans. They should try everything possible before suggesting major changes.

- Bullying happens but schools today are more aware. Report it when you see it and help your child develop some strategies to cope.

- School refusal needs careful handling. Work out the triggers and create a gradual return plan that suits your child.

- Sometimes mainstream schooling stops working for your child. Know your options and don't be afraid to make changes if needed.

CHAPTER 10

YOU

Throughout this book, I have focused primarily on discussing the child – their education, their supports, their social development. But in this final chapter, I want to turn the spotlight onto you, the parent. Because in the midst of IEP meetings, therapy appointments and advocacy efforts, it's easy to forget that your wellbeing matters too.

The journey of parenting a child with additional needs while navigating mainstream education is demanding in ways that others may never fully understand. It requires emotional resilience, physical stamina and mental fortitude that you might not have known you possessed before beginning this path. Some days you feel like a superhero, successfully juggling all the moving parts of your child's complex life. Other days, you might feel overwhelmed by the weight of responsibility and the constant need to push against systems not designed for your child.

For me, finding balance has been an ongoing process of adjustment and readjustment. There have been times when I have poured everything into supporting my child, only to realise I was running on empty. I have learned – sometimes the hard way – that taking care of myself isn't selfish; it's necessary. I have discovered that acknowledging my grief doesn't diminish my gratitude, and that asking for help is a sign of strength, not weakness.

This chapter explores strategies for maintaining your own mental health, finding balance between grief and gratitude, building your support network and remembering that amidst all the roles you play – case manager, advocate, therapist, parent – you are still you, with your own needs, interests and identity.

Better mindset, better outcome

There is a strong connection between mindset and health outcomes, supported by decades of research in behavioural medicine. When people believe in their ability to improve their health and view challenges as opportunities for growth, rather than obstacles, they tend to have lower stress, better immune function and faster recovery from illness. The power of mindset extends beyond individual health behaviours to shape how people with health challenges seek support and engage with healthcare providers, which leads to better health outcomes.

I believe this to be true when it comes to parenting and mainstreaming your special-needs child. The better my mindset is regarding his school experiences, teachers and progress, the better the outcome is.

I am not trying to sugar-coat the difficulty in parenting a special-needs child, but I have absolutely witnessed positive changes in my child's outcomes and experiences when my resilience and mindset are strong. And when my mindset is strong, I can encourage him to see his situation differently, too, which seems to serve him well. Does this mean I sometimes smile through gritted teeth, or smile when I could cry? Yes. But I will also clearly advocate at every opportunity and do everything to support my child, his teacher and the school to educate him.

Grief and gratitude

In a special-needs family, grief and gratitude often sit side by side. It is a messy, beautiful life of contradictions that's almost impossible to explain to others who are not experiencing it.

It's okay to feel sad for the life you thought you would have, while seeing the magic in what you have got.

Many parents of special-needs children connect with Emily Perl Kingsley's powerful 1987 essay 'Welcome to Holland', where she compares having a child with special needs to planning a trip to Italy but landing in Holland instead. Just as travellers must adjust their expectations from Roman architecture and Italian cuisine to tulips and windmills, parents of children with special needs must navigate the grief of letting go of preconceived expectations while discovering different, yet meaningful, experiences. This grief can be complex and cyclical, resurfacing at various developmental stages or life transitions, as families process not just the initial diagnosis but the ongoing adjustments to their families' unique journey.

Gratitude often emerges as a transformative force, helping families recognise and celebrate their unique experiences, strengths and connections. Many families report discovering deeper appreciation for small achievements, developing greater empathy and understanding, and finding joy in unexpected moments. The practice of gratitude doesn't diminish the challenges they face, but rather helps create a more balanced perspective, allowing them to acknowledge both the difficulties and the gifts of their journey.

When grief and gratitude interact, they often create a dynamic balance: the grief of certain challenges or lost expectations can co-exist with genuine gratitude for the unique perspectives, relationships and experiences that being a part of the special-needs community brings to family life. This interplay helps families develop resilience and find meaning in their distinctive path, much like discovering the unique beauty of Holland while still acknowledging the initial dream of Italy.

If you haven't read 'Welcome to Holland', do.

PARENT INSIGHT

Our firstborn daughter Rebecca has Down syndrome and recently turned 32. In the blink of an eye, we have found ourselves in 'the future' we always feared: older age, an emptier nest and retirement.

Fear of the future looms large for most parents raising a child with a disability, often overshadowing the small, everyday moments that bring joy and fulfillment. Our anxiety stemmed from concerns about Rebecca's long-term wellbeing, educational needs and her eventual independence.

Looking back on our journey, we spent too much time comparing Rebecca with her peers and fearing the future, which often robbed us of day-to-day joy. We have learned that you can try your best to navigate the journey, but don't always have control of the final destination. It is important to savour the simple joys of shared laughter, the small triumphs of mastering new skills, and the deep connections forged in moments of togetherness along the way. The secret is to balance forward thinking with an appreciation of the present, finding beauty in the everyday and embracing your unique journey.

The future feels good; the journey prepared us well for it.

Warwick Teale
Father to adult daughter with Down syndrome

Wellbeing

The analogy of putting on your own oxygen mask first – just as in airplane safety instructions – is particularly apt for parents of children with special needs. Most parents initially pour all their energy into supporting their child, researching therapies, attending appointments and advocating for their child, often at the expense of their own wellbeing. However, this approach can lead to burnout, exhaustion and diminished capacity to provide the sustained care and support their child needs. Just as an oxygen-deprived parent cannot effectively help their child with an oxygen mask, a depleted parent struggles to provide optimal support for their child's needs.

Creating space for self-care is not just beneficial, but essential. This might mean scheduling regular respite care, maintaining physical health through exercise and proper nutrition (yep, I know … eye roll), protecting sleep schedules and, most importantly, nurturing your mental health through counselling and connecting with your village.

Finding friends outside the special-needs community who can offer a listening ear without advice or judgement provides crucial emotional relief – a chance to process your feelings and experiences. I know many parents who have a few friends who support them in this way.

Some parents find that maintaining connections to their pre-diagnosis interests and friendships helps preserve their sense of identity beyond their caring role, too. Personally, I live for the once-a-term brunch dates I have with two other special-needs mums which I mentioned in chapter 8. We laugh; we cry; we share. Find what works for you and what gives you a chance to be yourself, among everything else going on.

The journey to prioritising wellbeing and self-care often involves working through guilt and the feeling that any time spent on yourself is time taken away from supporting your child. However, when parents maintain their own wellbeing, they can show up more fully and sustainably for their children. They also model healthy wellbeing and self-respect, while having more emotional and physical resources to navigate the challenges ahead.

While supporting their children, some parents begin to recognise familiar patterns in themselves or their partners. In some cases, this leads to the realisation that they too are neurodivergent – perhaps with undiagnosed ADHD, autism or other neurological differences. This discovery can be both illuminating and challenging. On one hand, it explains so much about your own life experiences; on the other, it means processing a new identity while already navigating your child's needs. If you find yourself in this situation, know that understanding your own neurodivergence can be a powerful tool for connecting with your child and advocating more effectively. It can also be an important step towards addressing your own needs and wellbeing.

PARENT INSIGHT

Parenting is a journey – any parent can tell you that. But the journey is a bit different with neurodiversity thrown into the mix. The road is windier, it can be darker at times, and there are often surprising twists and turns. Sometimes we feel as though we are walking blindfolded in the dark.

There are also unexpected pockets of light, rainbows of radical discovery, and a bright, somewhat different path leading forwards.

Discovering your own neurodiversity as a parent often follows a familiar trajectory. Your child is diagnosed, similar behaviours are present in both of you, and at some point you begin to question your neurotype. There can be doubt, grief, impostor syndrome and uncertainty along the way. Navigating this path is best done with an open heart and mind.

As parents of neurodiverse children, we often put our own needs on the backburner; but getting a diagnosis for yourself can be a wonderful step towards meeting your own needs.

Neurodiverse adults, women in particular, have likely learned to mask or suppress their sensory and other needs in various ways. If you have the option to learn what these needs are and meet them, it will not only enrich the journey you are on in understanding your child but will help you to become a calmer and more capable parent.

If you are interested in getting your own diagnosis of neurodiversity, a GP could be the first stop. Choose your GP carefully, as it's possible you will be met with doubt and disbelief. Medical understanding of neurodiversity can be very narrow and outdated. If you are able to access a neuro-affirming psychologist, they will provide the best support in pursuing a diagnosis as an adult. Sometimes a referral is not needed. There are many options available online, although wait times can be long.

Receiving a diagnosis of neurodivergence as an adult brings a barrage of emotions, similar to those experienced when a child is diagnosed. Suddenly so many things make perfect sense. It's as though there are doors in your mind that have been locked your entire life, and finally you have the keys.

It will help your neurodiverse child to love and accept themselves if they see their parent (or parents!) embracing their own neurodiversity. Not only this, but you and your child can learn to advocate for your needs and avoid misunderstanding and future mental health issues. Masking (concealing traits of neurodiversity) can have disastrous effects if maintained over time, and by helping our children to be themselves and promoting acceptance this can be avoided. By proudly promoting diversity acceptance, we can help create a better world for our children and ourselves.

Emily Furze-Smith
Neurodiverse mother

Expressing gratitude to your village

Expressing gratitude enriches daily life and strengthens connections with those around us. Taking time to appreciate the positive influences in our lives can create ripples of goodwill that benefit everyone.

There are many people other than us, their parents, who support our children. For many teachers and allied health professionals, working with students who have disabilities or special needs is more than a job – it is a calling. When educators, school staff and allied health professionals connect with and nurture our children, our children feel valued and appreciated, which helps them thrive.

Showing gratitude to your child's educators and support people not only acknowledges their dedication but also strengthens the vital partnership between you. A simple thank you (verbal or in a note) can make a profound difference. Flowers and food work well, too. Fostering positive relationships through an attitude of gratitude will ultimately benefit your child and their learning journey.

Educators often become an integral part of a family's support network. They share in the achievements and challenges along the way. Many maintain connections long after their formal teaching role ends, celebrating milestones and continuing to show genuine care for their former students' progress. A good teacher's impact can extend far beyond the classroom. As Andy Hargreaves says, 'Teachers who believe they can make a real difference in their students' lives really do.'

Chapter summary

- Having a positive mindset isn't about sugar-coating – it is about building resilience while still being a strong advocate for your child.

- Learn to balance grief and gratitude. It is okay to feel sad about the path that has closed while experiencing unexpected joy in different moments.

- Put your oxygen mask on first. Looking after yourself isn't selfish, it's essential for being there for your child long-term.

- Show thanks to those amazing teachers and support people who go above and beyond. Gratitude strengthens partnerships and helps everyone thrive.

- Remember you are doing a great job. It's a journey.

CONCLUSION

Even though primary school lasts for seven years, the time passes remarkably quickly. Before you know it, you will be thinking about the next step in the journey. One moment you are nervously walking your child through those school gates for the first time, and the next you are trying to work out where to send them for high school.

The journey moves at its own pace – sometimes frustratingly slow, other times alarmingly fast. High school will be a whole new adventure for families like ours. Different support structures, new social dynamics and changing expectations await. It might even become the subject of another book entirely.

Throughout these chapters, I have explored what it takes to successfully navigate mainstream primary schooling with a special-needs child. I have discussed knowing your rights, setting meaningful goals, creating a supportive team, working with professionals, managing the daily logistics, finding your community, weathering the inevitable tough times and – perhaps most importantly – taking care of yourself through it all.

These years have taught me the importance of advocacy, organisation and persistence. But they have also shown me the power of gratitude, of adjusting expectations and of celebrating the unique journey that mainstream primary schooling can offer.

I am trying to slow it all down now. To stay present in the primary school moments. Enjoy the walk to school each day. Appreciate the friends he is making. Celebrate everything he learns.

I am learning to live more comfortably with our unknown future while trusting that whatever challenges arise, we have the tools and experience to face them.

Like every parent, what I want most is a happy child. One who feels heard, understood and supported. One who knows they are loved unconditionally for exactly who they are.

I hope this book has served as the cheerleader I promised in the introduction – the voice telling you that, yes, mainstream primary schooling your special-needs child is possible if that is the path you choose. The rewards can be immeasurable.

The future remains unwritten, and I am still learning to embrace that uncertainty. Remember this: mainstream primary schooling a special-needs child is a hard job, and you will need to do it your way. There's no perfect formula or one-size-fits-all approach. But as you navigate this path with love, persistence and dedication, know that you are doing a great job. Even on the hardest days, especially on the hardest days, you are exactly the parent your child needs.

REFERENCES

Dimmitt, Melanie. (2019). *Special: Parenting when your child has a disability*. Ventura Press.

Field, Evelyn. (2023). *Bully Blocking: Empowering students to manage bullying*. Amba Press.

Fuller, Andrew. (2024). *Tricky Kids: A survival guide for parents*. Amba Press.

Henderson, Anna & Berla, Nancy (1994). *A new generation of evidence: The family is critical to student achievement*. National Committee for Citizens in Education.

Hooper, Judith. (2005). The difficult parent. *Special Educational Needs Magazine. https://senmagazine.co.uk/personal-stories/1862/the-difficult-parent/*

Kingsley, Emily. (1987). Welcome to Holland. *Sesame Street Parents, Fall 1987*.

Oberthur, Andrew. (2021) *Are You Ready for School?: Trust, collaboration and enquiry between parents and teachers.* Amba Press.

Russell, Dominique. (2022, 27 September). Being Taught by the Same Teacher Twice: The impact on achievement and behaviour. *Teacher Magazine.* https://www.teachermagazine.com/au_en/articles/being-taught-by-the-same-teacher-twice-the-impact-on-achievement-and-behaviour

KEY CONTACTS

Association for Children with Disability (ACD): *www.acd.org.au*

Children and Young People with Disability Australia (CYDA): *www.cyda.org.au*

Australian Human Rights Commission: *www.humanrights.gov.au*

Each state and territory in Australia has its own disability services oversight:

- Australian Capital Territory: *www.hrc.act.gov.au*
- New South Wales: *www.dcj.nsw.gov.au*
- Northern Territory: *www.hcscc.nt.gov.au*
- Queensland: *www.publicguardian.qld.gov.au*
- South Australia: *www.hcscc.sa.gov.au*
- Tasmania: *www.publicguardian.tas.gov.au*
- Victoria: *www.odsc.vic.gov.au*
- Western Australia: *www.hadsco.wa.gov.au*

ABOUT THE AUTHOR

Alicia Cohen is an educational publisher and mother of two, whose journey into advocacy began when her child was diagnosed. A seasoned writer of online articles, Alicia combines her professional background in educational publishing and her lived experience to create the resources she wishes she had during her own path of supporting a child with additional needs in a mainstream school setting. An avid reader of parenting literature and an experienced advocate, Alicia offers practical guidance for parents embarking on similar journeys through the mainstream education system.

www.ingramcontent.com/pod-product-compliance
Lightning Source LLC
Chambersburg PA
CBHW052048070526
44584CB00017B/2103